G E N E V A

Z U R I C H

⊡ B A S E L ⊡

GENEVA
ZURICH
⊞ BASEL ⊞

· HISTORY · CULTURE ·
& NATIONAL IDENTITY

NICOLAS BOUVIER

GORDON A. CRAIG

LIONEL GOSSMAN

WITH AN INTRODUCTION BY

CARL E. SCHORSKE

PRINCETON UNIVERSITY PRESS · PRINCETON, NEW JERSEY

Copyright © 1994 by Princeton University Press
Published by Princeton University Press, 41 William Street,
Princeton, New Jersey 08540
In the United Kingdom: Princeton University Press,
Chichester, West Sussex

Library of Congress Cataloging-in-Publication Data

Bouvier, Nicolas
Geneva, Zurich, Basel: history, culture, and national identity / Nicolas Bouvier,
Gordon A. Craig, Lionel Gossman; with an introduction by Carl E. Schorske.
p.   cm.
ISBN 0-691-03618-7
1. National characteristics, Swiss—Congresses.   2. Geneva (Switzerland)—
Civilization—Congresses.   3. Zurich (Switzerland)—Civilization—
Congresses.   4. Basel (Switzerland)—Civilization—Congresses.
I. Craig, Gordon Alexander, 1913–   . II. Gossman, Lionel.   III. Title.
DQ36.B63   1994
949.4—dc20   93-38138

Publication of this book has been aided by Pro Helvetia

This book has been composed in Adobe Caslon

· CONTENTS ·

· LIST OF ILLUSTRATIONS ·

THE THREE CITY STUDIES in this volume were originally presented at a colloquium on the topic "Cultural Unity and Diversity: Switzerland after 700 Years," which was held at the University of Southern California on March 15, 1991. Sponsored by the Pro Helvetia Foundation and the Max Kade Institute for Austrian-German-Swiss Studies, the Colloquium was intended to mark the seven hundredth anniversary of the Swiss Confederation. The introduction, by Carl E. Schorske, was written later.

The authors of the three studies were unknown to each other before the colloquium and wrote independently. Two are American university professors: one a professor of French literature at Princeton, the other a distinguished historian of Germany at Stanford. (Both, coincidentally, are natives of Glasgow, Scotland.) The third is a well-known Swiss essayist and writer of travel and ethnographic memoirs. Despite differences in style and the absence of prior consultation, several common themes run through the three studies. One is the tension in Swiss society, and in particular in the three city cultures examined here, between—on the one hand—the individual initiative, enterprise, and imagination to which all three cities have owed their survival and prosperity as independent polities, and—on the other—the strict codes of behavior they have imposed on their citizens in order to maintain their identity and independence against external and internal pressures. All three cities have both fostered and sought to discipline originality and eccentricity. Baselers, Genevans, and Zurichers have dealt with this tension in different ways, as the authors of the essays suggest. Many citizens found appropriate outlets for their creativity and imagination in business or diplomacy, science and scholarship. Others invented original ways of resolving the tension that have been influential far beyond the boundaries of their native cities and of Switzerland itself. With fewer inhabitants than Chicago, Switzerland has made a mark on the world out of all proportion to its population not only through gifted individual artists and intellectuals, such as Rousseau, Burckhardt, Karl Barth, Klee, Le Corbusier, and Giacometti, but through giant international business corporations like Nestlé of Vevey or Hoffmann Laroche and CIBA-Geigy of Basel and through international political or humanitarian institutions such as the Red Cross. A fair number of citizens of our three cities chose, however, to live in exile, or resorted to extreme forms of *dépaysement*. Some were destroyed or went mad. It cannot be said that the strong local identity to which Schorske refers in his introduction was maintained easily or without pain.

But it is the remarkable creation of a state unlike any of the great state formations of early modern Europe that distinguishes Switzerland. And it is the character of that state, the particular way each of the three cities has helped to maintain and develop it while at the same time preserving its own autonomous identity, and the lessons we can learn today from that political and cultural achievement that Schorske explores with economy and insight in his introduction. Schorske shows how the three cities, each with its own cultural character, economy, history, and fiercely defended autonomy, had to work out a relationship to the Swiss Confederation. All three joined the Confederation for reasons of security. But each of the three, having different interests and traditions, developed a different relation to it and sought to strike the right balance for itself between local autonomy and federal authority. As a result, the history of the Confederation has been one of recurrent tensions and even frictions. The need to moderate these led, however, to the development, over the years, of a refined art of continuous negotiation and compromise, which became fundamental to the very existence of the Swiss state. In Switzerland, in Schorske's words, "the ultimate source of sovereignty rests neither in the individual citizen nor in some central universal principle, but in the will of the autonomous communities."

In recent years doubts have been expressed in Switzerland itself about the viability of the Confederation. As Europe has changed, the Swiss have seemingly become disoriented. Many of them no longer feel sure what it means to be Swiss. Eminent Swiss writers have denounced their country's image of itself as a hypocritical charade. When Vaclav Havel received a literary prize in Zurich in November 1990, Friedrich Dürrenmatt gave his last public speech before his death. To the consternation of those present, he compared Switzerland to a prison: "Since everybody else outside this prison was at each other's throat and since only in their prison do the Swiss feel secure from assault, they feel free, freer than other people, free as prisoners in the prison of their neutrality." Shortly afterwards, Max Frisch refused to take part in the celebration of the seven-hundredth anniversary and took care to see that at his death he would not be recuperated as an ornament of the state. The recent referendum on association with the EEC, to which Schorske refers at the end of his introduction, has aggravated what appears to be a fairly serious crisis of identity.

This crisis is closely related to the disjunction in Switzerland of culture and nationality, and it is felt most keenly by writers, artists, and intellectuals. In the opinion of Etienne Barilier, who hails from French-speaking canton Vaud, "the more detached a Swiss person is from the world of culture, the more he feels comfortably Swiss; the more he lives in the world of art and the mind, the more uncertain his identity." It may be true that Switzerland has achieved the miracle for which it is generally admired: namely, replacing central authority, which dominates and oppresses minorities, with the mutual cooperation of the country's constituent regions and entities. But it has done so at a price. "If the minorities (in particular the diverse languages and cultures) are not oppressed in Switzerland, it is essentially because, of their own accord, they spontaneously renounce existing too intensely, manifesting themselves as 'a people.' They practice self-censorship." Hence the concern not to *stand out* that is perfectly internalized in Switzerland for individuals as well as groups. Cultural energies, in other words, may not take on a national dimension as they do in countries like France. They are *in* the country, as Barilier puts it, but they are not *of* it. They do not define it. The result is that Switzerland is "the place of cultural regulation, not the place of culture." Culture is what Switzerland prides itself on "respecting," not what constitutes it as a country.

These are serious criticisms. They strike a particularly urgent note in the midst of our own debates on "multiculturalism." What it means to be Swiss when one's culture is predominantly French or German or Italian is a question not wholly unlike what it means to be American when one's culture is Hispanic or Jewish or black. At issue is the relation of cultural identity and political identity. Barilier believes that writers and artists would like cultural identity to take precedence over national identity. At the same time, he insists that no writer or artist wants to see culture become the basis of another political entity, another set of frontiers. "While we may truly define ourselves by a culture more than by a nation, we would never want to turn our culture into a nation." In this respect, he concludes, artists and writers born in Switzerland—"since they live in a country that cannot be a culture, and in a culture that cannot be their nation"—have a special perspective on the world. What they see is that the cultural is not and in fact should not be completely identical with the political, that the state should be honored for the political achievement that it is, but should not be expected or permitted to overstep its boundaries. That is a strikingly Burckhardtian piece of wisdom. Perhaps there's something to being Swiss after all.[1]

✦ ✦ ✦

The contributors wish to express their thanks to the Pro Helvetia Foundation and the Max Kade Foundation, to the organizers of the colloquium, Professors Albert Sonnenfeld and Cornelius Schnauber, and to Dean Marshall Cohen and the University of Southern California for their generous interest and hospitality. In addition, the

---

[1] On the Swiss "identity crisis," see the special number of *The Literary Review* entitled "Post Festum: Switzerland and the World" (Summer 1993), in particular the articles by Rolf Kieser (pp. 437–45), Pier Giorgio Conti (pp. 468–77), Etienne Barilier (pp. 508–11), and Hugo Loetscher (pp. 532–37).

three original authors are indebted to Carl Schorske for having written an introduction that draws their autonomous essays together in a loose, yet functional confederation and reveals not only their common themes but the continuing cultural and political interest and pertinence of the Swiss experiment. In a year that began with the breakup of Czechoslovakia and may not see the end of the carnage in what is now referred to as "the former Yugoslavia," the Helvetic Confederation deserves our respectful attention.

LIONEL GOSSMAN
Princeton, September 1993

GENEVA

———————————

ZURICH

———————————

◼ BASEL ◼

INTRODUCTION

Carl E. Schorske

Are we living through a Swiss moment in European history? Since the end of the Second World War, the nations of Western Europe, sated with the terrors of history, have been groping for an institutional framework strong enough to protect them against themselves and against powers even mightier. Yet that framework must be loose enough to allow the autonomy of each participant to flourish. It is a road that Switzerland travelled before them. A microcosm of Europe, with its divisions of nationality, religion, economy, and regional culture, Switzerland took seven hundred years to achieve its supranational federal state. Yet now, when Europe bids fair to becoming a macrocosm of Switzerland, Europe's unity puts that country's basic political achievement at risk. Europe's Swiss moment as it struggles toward its unity is also Switzerland's European moment. The little state is challenged to abandon the existential premises—total autonomy and neutrality—on which its freedom and its pluralistic polity have rested.

The Swiss Confederation was created not to become a "nation-state," but to protect and foster the autonomy of its constituent parts, the cantons. How different was its formation from that of the great states of Europe! They were built largely from above, by the expansion of feudal-aristocratic power into princely, then into royal, territorial power. In England, France, and Spain, feudalism was dissolved from above by monarchs who in their process of centralization gradually destroyed the local powers and their particular rights and immunities. In Switzerland, by contrast, feudalism was dissolved from below. Local peasants, urban artisans, and merchants, in sporadic, largely separate struggles, expanded their communal powers at the expense of their aristocratic or ecclesiastical territorial overlords. In this process, and to safeguard their liberties against ever larger neighboring states, the Swiss communities learned to band together as associated communes. First in loose, temporary alliances, then in stronger leagues (some of which reached well beyond what is now Switzerland), the Swiss communes pursued in an almost unconscious political way a cellular method of state building. Each local entity became associated with others in a unity of difference, alienating only as little power as was necessary to defend and preserve each member's particularity.

The nucleus of this associative development was formed in the mountain valleys of eastern Switzerland. There geography favored the development of both armed collaboration and market cooperation against local lords and foreign overlords. Three of these "forest places"—ancestors of the cantons—joined together at Rütli in 1291 in a solemn oath to defend their right to control law and justice in their valleys. To this day, Switzerland calls itself an *Eidgenossenschaft* (oath cooperative) after the assembly of Rütli, with the same implication that its bonding exists for the defense of the particular liberties of each against outsiders. Identity is in the local part, protection in the collective whole.

During the fourteenth century, in a context of weakening feudalism and expanding trade, some of the newly developing cities joined the valley communes to expand the nuclear league into a union of "eight places." With the increase of trade and crafts, the urban guilds joined the valley communes in their struggles against feudal lords, winning from them, whether by arms or by purchase, their rights to self-government. It was a stormy process, with conflicts among the communities themselves often as bitter as those against older rulers. It was in this context that Zurich, though often rent by social discord within, expanded both its political and its economic power over its neighbors to emerge as a major dynamic factor in Swiss politics. It did not, however, become a dominant centralizing power as did the aggrandizing territorial princes in neighboring states. Swiss integration was accomplished without a Castille, a Piedmont, or a Prussia, without a unifying power that could impose its regional will and its stamp upon the whole.

Swiss geography and geopolitics both allowed and sustained a tension-laden yet effective polycentricity. With stubborn insistence on their autonomy, the cantons canalized all attempts at state building into the associative mode of a league rather than the centralizing mode of the unitary state. Consequently the Swiss polity is, in Jonathan Steinberg's apt term, "bottom-heavy." The ultimate source of sovereignty rests neither in the individual citizen nor in some central universal principle, but in the will of the autonomous communities. At the practical level, this has come to mean the canton. When the canton cannot satisfy the grievances of its subcommunities, or sustain good relations with other cantons, the Confederation will intervene with diplomacy or with various forms of pressure to create some new modus vivendi among contending parties. As a consequence of its associative genealogy, the very constitution of Switzerland is strikingly flexible. Indeed, it is probably the most amendable constitution in the world, like an ever-renegotiable contract among its autonomous members. Switzerland achieves stability not so much by fixity of principle or enduring division of powers in its central institutions, as by the adjustability of the constitution through an easy use of referenda in the face of new historical forces that threaten the health of the *Genossenschaft*, the national community. The federal government is the guarantor of regionally organized difference not only against external threats but also against central domination and internal disruption.

✦ ✦ ✦

The historical process of cellular association that produced Switzerland's polycentric polity has lent a special significance to the Swiss city. Despite the presence of interests, institutions, and even cultural characteristics that all Swiss citizens have come slowly to share, their cultural identity remains anchored to an astonishing degree in the local city or canton. Until very recently, one of the two newspapers of Basel was entitled the *Baseler Nationalzeitung*. The word "national" in that title referred not to Switzerland but to little Basel. As

Lionel Gossman points out in his essay on that city, Baselers, when
they left their canton, until quite recently spoke of "going to Switzerland." In Geneva it was no different, so Nicolas Bouvier tells us: until
about 1920, "la nation" meant Geneva; Switzerland was "la patrie."
Of course a Swiss patriotism is real enough, bred as it is of a pride in
the country's successful confrontation of the terrors of history with
institutions and actions shaped and reshaped to preserve rather than
to flatten the differences among the constituent communities. Yet
precisely for that reason, the cities and communes of Switzerland
remain, as perhaps nowhere else in Europe, vital centers of cultural
identity. They give social and cultural substance to the maintenance
of difference in their polycentric nation.

To examine the cities of Switzerland as this volume does is to
study aspects or faces of the country as a whole—a country that,
culturally and civically, remains paradoxically less than the sum of its
parts. Switzerland boasts no great metropolis as its capital—no Paris,
London, or Berlin. What a modest city is Bern, that serves the loose-
knit federation as its political center! Bern won its status as capital
out of its centuries of vigorous participation in the often-military
struggles of Swiss integration and defense. Politically it is *primus
inter pares*, but it exercises no dominance over the other larger cities.
All participate in different ways in the multifaceted transnational
state, giving it their color and cultural character. Perhaps one can
best understand Swiss cities as rough Lilliputian equivalents of the
nations in a Europe that is still to be united.

For the three cities in this study—Zurich, Basel, and Geneva—
the era of the Reformation remains in the half-light of memory as a
defining moment of civic identity. It was then that each city-state
developed its own way of relating to modern Switzerland: Zurich as
militant organizer; Basel, as irenic, cosmopolitan mediator; Geneva,
as radiating center of legal and ethical principles of international
behavior. However transformed in the processes of modernization
and secularization, these characteristics of each city persisted deep
into the nineteenth century and continue to resonate even to the

present day. They are embodied too in the very different sixteenth-century culture-heroes: Zwingli of Zurich, Erasmus of Basel, and Calvin of Geneva. Each of these men, far-reaching in their European influence, established particular connections between religion, culture, and power that were congenial to the formation of the modern identities of their respective city-states.

Huldrych Zwingli, Zurich's militant religious reformer, yoked religion to political power for the conversion of the whole Swiss Confederation to the new faith. When the Catholic cantons resisted it, Zwingli and his Zurich led the Protestant forces in their attempt to impose their faith by arms. Zwingli lost his life in the defeat that ensued, leaving the Confederation, never very tight, weakened as it entered upon centuries of intercantonal religious strife. Even in the nineteenth century, religious difference produced a secession from the Confederation by Catholic cantons whose autonomy was threatened by liberal and Protestant revolutionaries. Zurich once again took up the role it had in Zwingli's time, that of political-military spearhead of ideological uniformity—this time, a liberal-secular uniformity—to undergird the Confederation against the secession of the Catholic cantons. Gordon Craig's account of Zurich in the nineteenth century centers strongly on the novelist Gottfried Keller, who also became something of a culture hero to his city. In the spirit of Zwingli, he integrated moral commitment and ideological zeal (in this case liberal rather than religious) with political skill. Reforming the city government, Keller expanded Zurich's role in Switzerland, enhancing the power of the Confederation against the Catholic cantons. Zurich's culture-heroes were thus both exemplars of the intellectual activist, harnessing their vigorous idealism to the realities of politics. They embodied well the creative, if often aggressive, centralizing role that their city played in the modernization of Switzerland.

How different were the equivalent culture-heroes of Basel! Desiderius Erasmus in the sixteenth century, Jacob Burckhardt in the nineteenth—these were not men of action, but scholars and humanists. They prized wisdom over smarts. They viewed with skeptical reserve the combination of moral passion and political will that moved their respective Zurich contemporaries, Zwingli and Keller. Such too was the temper of the Basel patriciate, a ruling class that sought its security and civic autonomy not through expansive action, but through prudent economic dealings, evasive political action, and peaceful diplomacy. As Lionel Gossman shows, Basel cultivated humanistic culture not only for its intrinsic value, but also to school its elite in a cosmopolitan spirit, a sophisticated understanding for the ways of others as a means of survival and maneuver in a pluralistic world of powers too great for a small, exposed polis to control. Basel's patricians, while they maintained a dogged, local, civic exclusivism, acquired an easy command of Europe's cultures that, then as now, served their commercial and political interests well. Even Erasmus, with his European prestige, promoted not only intellectual life. He was also a major figure in an economically significant culture industry that involved printers, scholars, artists, and entrepreneurs. When the city was swept into the Protestant camp, humanism maintained some atmosphere of moderation in Basel. So it was that Erasmus, who remained a Catholic, could return after a brief exile to resume his work in the city. Basel's university, a center of primary civic importance, provided even in the heated sixteenth century a scene for critical, independent scholars, such as the Savoyard theorist of tolerance, Sebastian Castellio, to convert the poison of religious strife into the elixir of intellectual understanding.

In the nineteenth century, in the face of the forces of liberalism, democracy, and centralized state power vigorously espoused for Switzerland by Zurich, Basel's patriciate fought in vain to maintain its local privileges and traditional culture. Jacob Burckhardt, the founder of modern cultural history, lifted to view the value-creations of the past against the modern "illusions" of progressive politics and modern concentrations of power. Like the great families of Basel whence he sprang, he defended traditional cantonal rights—even of Catholics—against the liberal centralizers of the 1840s. As for his scholarly vocation, it was at once narrowly civic and broadly cosmopolitan. Burckhardt would serve Basel by making its citizens, through history, aware of the plurality of cultures and understanding of their differences. Thus, he would prepare the city's elite youth to live richly and skillfully in a world too complex to control. At the same time Burckhardt's work was dedicated to the Europeans as a whole, to preserve and defend their inherited culture as a value in itself against the terrible simplifiers and power brokers of modern society.

The founding father of a renewed Geneva in the Reformation era, John Calvin, synthesized politics and religion no less effectively than his great contemporary in Zurich, Huldrych Zwingli. A lawyer by training and a theocrat by conviction, Calvin was not content like Zwingli to stamp out ecclesiastical and civic corruption. He aimed also to bring every aspect of community life under the law of God. Logical clarity and rational discipline were his instruments with which to define and promote institutional and ethical order. Geneva was to serve as a radiating center of godliness.

In the long process of secularization, Geneva's religious righteousness slowly became transmuted into a creative concern for political rights and the extension of the rule of law. Nicolas Bouvier in his essay on Geneva reminds us not only of the little republic's radical theorist of political rights, Jean-Jacques Rousseau, but also of Henry Dunant, the founder of the International Red Cross, an institution that has become a veritable symbol of the Swiss contribution to mankind. Dunant's strategy to relieve human suffering—from wounded soldiers to civilian victims of catastrophes of man and nature—was, not unlike Calvin's, legal in its method, international in its scope, and institutional in its practical form. The Swiss government ultimately made Dunant's humanitarian cause its own. Sponsoring the conference that led to the first Geneva Convention, Switzerland took the first step in expanding international law to mitigate human suffering in armed conflict. The Red Cross, with its rational, ethical focus and its universality, may be viewed today as a pioneering model for our modern multinationals of the human interest, such as Amnesty International, Greenpeace, and the movements for nuclear disarmament. Following the strategy of Geneva's Dunant, those cosmopolitan movements realize their sharply defined ethical aims by a combination of moral agitation, practiced voluntary action, and impartial political pressure on the states to adopt their policies in the human interest, securing them by international agreements. The Helsinki Accords on human rights are but the most striking achievement of the transpolitical strategy in the creation of which Geneva played a formative role.

It is astonishing how our three cities, despite an increasing uniformity produced in them by modern centralization, industrialization, and democratization, maintained the contrasting characteristics that emerged in the era of their chosen culture-heroes. With respect to the Swiss state, Zurich remained the energetic centralizer as in the time of Zwingli. It led the liberal unionists in the Civil War of the 1840s, in the construction of the Federal State of 1848, and in the democratization of the constitution of 1874. Basel continued to be the cautious, anxious, and sometimes stubborn defender of her local city-state tradition and of patrician oligarchy. While never championing secession or disruption of the Confederation, the city fathers applied their not inconsiderable political and diplomatic skill to sustaining cantonal autonomy. Geneva realized its hope of joining the Swiss Confederation only after the defeat of Napoleon. Like Zurich, it was committed to strengthening the liberal, sometimes radical, character of the Confederation. Like Basel, it championed local autonomy, though largely in order to hold the hated Catholics at arm's length. Here modern radicalism took up the torch of principled, righteous intolerance from Calvinism. Not until 1907 were church and state separated in Geneva.

Our authors touch many of the same subjects in their urban portraits. They thus invite the reader to compare the three cities in many spheres of culture and society: education, scientific creativity, the arts and their patronage, the different kinds of refugees welcomed and the varied nature of their integration, the relation of each city to other countries, and—not least—the different foci of economic life in these vigorous centers of capitalism that have known how to adapt their very different traditions to modern conditions.

To cite but a single example of the comparative perspectives opened by our authors, let us take the place of universities in each city. In Basel, the university was charged to prepare the elite to face the multicultural world, its opportunities and dangers, with both cosmopolitan flexibility and a strong sense of local identity. The professors began to ground the students in the humanistic patrimony of "civicism" even in the preparatory school where university scholars were obliged to teach. Lionel Gossman shows how Basel refreshed its own academic humanism by welcoming refugees or dissidents from German reaction down to modern times. Often political radicals, the humanistic professors were nevertheless cultural conservatives like their Basel-born colleagues, revitalizing in innovative ways ancient values threatened in the modern world.

It is said that, if, in meeting a member of the Basel elite, you wish to please him, you should address him as "Herr Professor." A citizen of Zurich, however, you should call "Herr Direktor" (a director of a business firm). Yet Basel's professors usually came of business families. In the mid-nineteenth century, Zurich's business men wished to have a university too. More, they characteristically wished theirs to be a national university, serving all Switzerland. Basel, fearing centralized power as always, and in defense of its own university, opposed the new institution. A compromise was found: Zurich would establish a confederal technical university that, however, would offer humanistic instruction. German scholars were invited to teach in Zurich too, but they were of the mainstream of German academic learning, not intellectual resisters of modern civilization like the Germans appointed at Basel. As a full university, Zurich over the last century became a magnet for international avant-garde students. This too befit the metropolitan stature which, alone of our three cities, Zurich achieved.

In Geneva, Calvin had founded an academy to prepare ministers of the Word but also to educate citizens for political responsibility. Although the academy's faculty pursued the higher learning, the Company of Ministers that controlled it did not allow it to become a full-fledged university, lest it draw foreigners—especially Catholics—to Geneva. Refugees from France after 1685 helped to make it a strong center of Protestant enlightenment. Only in 1873 did the academy become a university. Strongly anchored in Geneva's Calvinist tradition of ethics, legality, and a concern for education, the university secularized its Calvinist tradition of rationalism to become a center of law and social science of European stature. The special quality of principled culture that Geneva brought to Switzerland's creative internationalist role in the modern world was fittingly paralleled and nurtured in its academic institutions. Where conservative, Epimethean Basel maintained in its intellectual community a humanistic piety for the past, and Promethean Zurich developed an openness to the scientific and artistic venturesomeness of a future-oriented European metropolis, Geneva nurtured its tradition of normative transcendence with a practical intent.

Though bourgeois cities all, in their three universities, with their striking cultural variety, they intellectualized the special aspects of a civic ethos that has enabled Switzerland to be more than a nation while remaining less than one, offering many ways of relating positively to the international power complex. Capitalizing on its own differences, dearly preserved in its universities, Switzerland has learned how to live in a world of difference. Through these and other symmetries in the accounts of our three cities the reader will be able to grasp their natures in comparative perspective.

✦ ✦ ✦

It is our good fortune that each author is by temperament and intellectual commitment peculiarly qualified to portray the city he has chosen. Gordon Craig has devoted much of his life of learning to nineteenth-century Germany, and especially to Prussia's role in the unification and transformation of that country. Concerned with the relation of liberalism, political power, and capitalism in Germany, Craig turns his attention to Zurich. Was not Zurich the driving power of centralization and modern state-building in Switzerland as Prussia was in Germany? The materialism of Zurich's Bahnhofs-strasse often clashed, as in Germany, with the liberal idealism of the intellectuals. But in Zurich, unopposed by a powerful neo-feudal force, capitalism and liberal idealism found an efficacious union, strengthening the city's centralist impulses to domination. These were curbed by the real power of Basel and the autonomist cantons, but Zurich remained the most vital energizer of Switzerland's political and economic modernization.

What better chronicler of Basel than Lionel Gossman? Profoundly concerned in our own world with the nature and vocation of the humanist scholar, he has long explored the antinomies and ambiguities of Europe's literary and historical intelligentsia over four centuries. He has shown how in Basel, the patrician "sulking-corner of Europe," some of the most innovative ideas about culture were the product of political defeat or frustration. If Gossman's analysis focuses strongly on the relation of humanistic and civic culture, that was the quintessential concern of the intelligentsia of Basel too, committed as it was to the service of the *respublica basiliensis*.

Nicolas Bouvier, himself a native of Geneva, and a world traveller and observer, has written among other works a study of Japan. In the strength of its conventions and the persistence of its highly codified civic ethos through the transformations that time has wrought, Japan's culture bears some kinship, distant yet fundamental, to Geneva. Bouvier's focus on legality and philanthropy, rationality and the quest for rights, as characteristic of his native city illuminates yet another variant of the bourgeois culture so richly represented in the Swiss Confederation.

The match of each author and the city that is his subject gives a striking sharpness to the three images. Yet we may wonder how our Helvetic triptych would appear if our authors had exchanged cities: what if Gordon Craig, with his sensitivity to power and ideology, had given us a portrait of the troubled communitarian humanists of

Basel; if Lionel Gossman had scrutinized the *Bahnhofstrasse* culture
and the unselfconscious, Promethean liberals who made Zurich the
modernizing spearhead of Switzerland; or if Nicolas Bouvier had
brought his structural, taxonomic perception of culture to bear upon
the dynamism of Zurich, or on the capacious, melancholy wisdom of
Basel? Fortified with the widely varied yet congruent perspectives of
the city culture each author has provided, it is open to the reader to
develop his or her own configuration of the vital urban entities that
have brought their unique and precious legacies to Swiss civilization.

That in the course of nation-building the three Swiss cities have
become more alike in social structure and in culture goes without
saying. Today, in the face of the great decision to join in the construction of a united Europe, Zurich, Basel and Geneva have shown
their like-mindedness in a resounding yes vote to entering the European Economic Area. But in Switzerland as a whole, they were on
the losing side in the crucial referendum of December 6, 1992. On
the question of the first modest step to European integration the
divisions in Swiss society—national, class, and regional—surfaced in
a majority "no" to Europe, a vote anchored in the traditions of Swiss
isolation and autonomy. While the French cantons voted for Europe, the German cantons (Basel excepted) voted against. Like other
European minority groups such as the Catalans or the Scots, the
French Swiss favored a European structure partly in order to curb the
dominant nationality. The German cantons, traditionally the seat of
Swiss patriotism, were favored by the "bottom-heavy" constitution,
and voted to preserve it against a fantasized European state. The
rural population reinforced the German vote for Swiss isolation,
while the urban electorate voted with the French for Europe.

In this context of resurgent Swiss localism, neutralism, and a
strong dash of xenophobia, our three cities were as one in supporting
entry into the European Economic Area. That economic considera-
tions and political realism played a dominant part in their disposition
to find Switzerland's fortunes in new European forms is scarcely
to be doubted. Yet the vote for Europe was, in terms of the cities'

deepest traditions, a logical projection of their special blends of cosmopolitanism and strong local identity. Zurich, leader in the making of the Swiss Confederation, could, as the country's vigorous metropolis, find a congenial field of action in a loosely unified Europe. Both Basel cantons, city and country, whose ties to all their European neighbors have always been cultivated with as much economic and cultural energy as the constellation of power among them allowed, voted—alone among the German cantons—to follow the European road. For Geneva, with her deep affinities to France and her firmly established position as a creative center of internationalism in theory and institutional practice, there could be no hesitation. Seventy-eight per cent of her voters chose entry into the European Economic Area.

All three cities, whose differences had long inhibited Switzerland's uniformity but ultimately enriched its polycentric culture, have reached the level of a shared cosmopolitan economic and political outlook, one that allows them to see their future welfare in a larger European unity. That unity in turn could realize on a grander scale the multicultural achievement of their country, to which each city has made its vital and distinctive contribution.

 GENEVA

Nicolas Bouvier

1. Geneva: Watchmakers' shops in Coutance

HISTORICALLY and geographically, Geneva is the least Swiss of the three cities evoked in this book. In sentiment, it is as Swiss as any other.

Last week, I was discussing the hackneyed problem of Swiss identity with Hugo Loetscher, the Zurich novelist and journalist. Which would come first, the question ran, Swiss or local patriotism? Loetscher said he did not care. I do. The Zurichers have been Swiss for six hundred years, since 1394 to be precise. My family has been Genevan for three hundred years and Swiss since 1814. That does make a difference, quantitatively if not qualitatively.

The cantons of Valais, Neuchâtel, and Geneva are latecomers to this Confederation, admitted at the eleventh hour. Yet Geneva had asked to join as a full-fledged member as early as 1572, in order to be protected against the Duke of Savoy. That was a few years after the treaty of Cateau-Cambresis, which left the Savoyards free to turn against Geneva. The answer, inspired by the Catholic cantons, was no. After the fall of Napoleon, Geneva asked again, supported this time by the Allies, particularly Russia and England, who wanted to make Switzerland a neutral but strong buffer state. Save for the Protestant cities of Bern, Basel, and Zurich, which had been allies or "combourgeois" since the fifteenth century, the Swiss were only mildly interested. They justly feared that this territorial expansion would complicate the linguistic pattern of the country and, above all, upset the religious balance between the confessions. With twenty-five thousand inhabitants in 1815, Geneva was by far the largest city in Switzerland and, in spite of the financial drain of the French occupation, still a rich one.

Still, the answer this time was a polite yes. The Genevans were overjoyed. For two and a half centuries they had been practically alone in defense of their independence and their theocracy. The general feeling was of gratitude and relief: in Vonnegut's phrase, "lonesome no more."

As far as political philosophy was concerned, moreover, Geneva had much in common with Switzerland. Joining was perhaps a choice imposed by circumstances, but it was also the best possible choice.

✦ ✦ ✦

At the western and southernmost tip of Swiss territory, Geneva looks like an artificial appendage. Mentally, if no longer physically, it is still a remote place for many German-speaking Confederates. I have come across numerous young German-speaking writers who had traveled the world over and never seen Geneva. I invited them: they loved it. We spoke English together, an absurd and typically Swiss situation. They felt ill at ease in *Schriftdeutsch*; I do not speak *Schwyzertutsch* and, since World War II, the French language has lost some of its presence and prestige among the elites of Western Europe, which is a shame and a pity.

The tiny and lovely territory of Geneva has a common border of only six miles with Switzerland, but its border with neighboring and encircling France extends for about a hundred. I suppose almost the same thing could be said of Basel or Schaffhausen. The main highway from Geneva to Lausanne, along the north side of the lake, is still known as *La route Suisse*, after its destination. As late as 1920, the word *nation* was used about Geneva, and the word *patrie* about Switzerland. That explains why, in Geneva, patriotic or chauvinist feeling is first local, then Swiss.

Is this to say that the Genevans are second-rate, tepid, or shamefaced Swiss? By no means. As we shall see, they have played a very active part in the affairs of the country. A few years ago a separatist movement was founded in Geneva, led by some brilliant young barristers who were outraged by the haughtiness and brutality of Zurich: an easily understandable reaction but, to me, no more than a youthful prank.

Although the contribution of cities like Basel or Zurich to European and world culture is as important (if not more important, at least in the realm of the fine arts) as that of Geneva, the name of Geneva is better-known abroad. It is certainly the only one of the three that an Ontario grocer or an Australian bus driver might be able to mark on the map without hesitation and without mistaking Switzerland for Sweden. This situation is due to such figures as Jean Calvin, Jean-Jacques Rousseau (*"enfant de Genève"*) and Henry Dunant, the father of the International Red Cross in the nineteenth century, as well as to such facts as the presence in Geneva of international organizations and of conferences on Vietnam, disarmament, Cambodia, and so on. When the big guns of world politics want to meet on neutral ground, it seems that Geneva is still the right place. At least that was the opinion expressed by former Secretary of State, George Shultz, in a speech at Stanford University in the spring of 1991.

Now if we wanted to take a closer look at the way Geneva has treated its most illustrious citizens, we should have to bear the following in mind:

—The Frenchman, Jean Calvin, was first invited by the Genevans, then expelled by them for abuse of authority, then urgently pressed to come back because the city was on the verge of moral and political collapse.

—Jean-Jacques Rousseau, the son of a Genevan watchmaker and a citizen of Geneva, was banished from his native city in spite, or because, of his genius and his liberal theories, and several of his works remained banned until the French invasion in 1798. He was later to exert a tremendous influence on Geneva's pedagogical tradition.

—Henry Dunant, the real founder and father of the International Red Cross was dismissed by his peers because he had declared bankruptcy (a deadly sin in a bankers' city). As a result, he had no part in the successful Geneva Conference of 1864, at which fourteen nations signed the Geneva Conventions for the Protection of Wounded Sol-

diers. When, much later, at the beginning of this century, Henry Dunant was awarded the first Nobel Peace Prize, the Red Cross had
become one of the best-known institutions in the world, and he, its
father, was living alone, entirely forgotten, in an old people's home at
Heiden in Canton Appenzell. In atonement and embarrassment, Geneva hastily printed a commemorative postage stamp bearing his portrait, and tried to bring him back to a more dignified life in Geneva.
He refused. Now there is both an Institut J.-J. Rousseau and an Institut Henry Dunant.

This not only proves that the Swiss are very good at recuperation
and that a part, at least, of their reputation is due to citizens who
were persecuted before they were granted a belated recognition; it
also establishes that Switzerland is really too small a country (not its
fault) for outstanding characters, and that real geniuses are too awk-
ward for such a well-monitored society. They have to disappear or go
away. This is Swiss, not just Genevan. After all, Zurich could not
keep Füssli; Basel could not keep Paracelsus; Neuchâtel could not
offer the mental space that would have been needed to retain Blaise
Cendrars and Edouard Jeanneret, alias Le Corbusier.

✦ ✦ ✦

As early as 58 B.C., in *The Gallic Wars* Julius Caesar mentions an
important settlement or town at the outlet of Lake Leman and a
wooden bridge of great strategic importance crossing the river
Rhone. There was no other bridge or ford to the south for more than
two hundred miles. The meaning of Geneva (Latin: Geneva), a Cel-
tic name, is still hotly disputed.

Taking advantage of its excellent geographic situation and of
centuries of *pax romana* and later *pax burgundia*, Geneva became a
prosperous fair-town and a bishopric linked to the neighboring
Duchy of Savoy—a destiny similar to that of hundreds of medieval
cities. Before we can really speak of a contribution to European
culture, we have to wait until the sixteenth century, the Age of the
Reformation, but for two exceptions that are worth mentioning:

a. A splendid triptych (oil on wood) by the itinerant German painter Conrad Witz in the late fifteenth century, representing the Miraculous Draft of Fishes. In the background, one can see a highly realistic view of the southern shore of Lake Geneva. Recognizable today, some young oak trees in Witz's painting are still standing, much bigger, five centuries older.

b. The first illustrated love story in occidental printing (as distinct from Korean printing, which began about fifty years earlier). It is a magnificent *incunabula*, dated 1483, with fifty-three hand-colored woodcuts, printed by Adam Steinschaber, who had left Gutenberg's atelier to settle in Geneva in 1472. Entitled *L'Histoire de la belle fée Mélusine*, it is the fairy tale of a mermaid (or, rather, a rivermaid) supposed to be the patron of the family of Lusignan, the Kings of Jerusalem, who surrendered the Holy City to their conqueror, the Kurdish general Sala-ud-Din (Saladin) in the late eleventh century. The book is elegant and original, a masterpiece of fifteenth-century graphics. Of an estimated three hundred copies, only two have survived: one in Geneva, one in Wolfenbüttel (Germany). It is the rarest printed book in the West today.

I mention these artistic landmarks as a kind of adieu. Geneva now leaves the gentle waters of fine arts and gallantry to sail toward the darker and stormier sea of militant Protestantism and the crusade for a new faith. For more than a century, the Genevan printers printed no more fairy tales or love stories.

✦ ✦ ✦

In 1536, Bern, converted to the Reformation, invades Canton Vaud, the territories of Chablais and Faucigny, and routs the Duke of Savoy, the age-old foe of Geneva.

The same year, on May 21, the *Grand Conseil* or General Council of Geneva—that is, the totality of citizens eligible for public office—adopts the new faith of the Reformation unanimously.

It is a political choice: Bern is a formidable military power and a traditional ally of Geneva. But it is even more a spiritual choice: for two years ministers of the Reform movement, sent by Bern, had been preaching in the town, confronting Catholic theologians in public disputes, and getting the better of them. They won because they offered a better, more bracing, and exciting message to listeners terrified by war, plague, and inquisition, and whose life expectancy (let us note) was around twenty-three years.

Nowadays, in our language, Calvinism evokes the most rigorous, tormented, and exacting approach to religion. Not so in 1536. In the Reform movement at its peak—whether Lutheran, Zwinglian, Calvinist, or French—there was a roaring, devastating jubilation that we can hardly imagine today but that the French historian Michelet, though an unbeliever, superbly recaptured in his chapter on the family of the French admiral Coligny.

At the turn of the sixteenth century the German humanist, polemicist, and soldier, Ulrich von Hutten, had written: "Ideas clash like spears; it's a pleasure to be alive." The message now became even more urgent and pointed: "God has returned to us and has brought us His Book" (Erasmus's and Luther's translations of the New Testament). This book, a source of hope and wisdom, should be open to every one, regardless of social status or sex. Thus, in the year 1536, school was made compulsory for all children in Geneva, with the help of a reading manual fresh from the printer's press, in which the sound of consonants, vowels, and syllables are explained by means of animal homophones, such as the bumblebee for *b* and *z* (*bzzz*) or the owl for *ou* (*hu hu*).

Even Jean Calvin, who had settled in Geneva in the same year (1536), was carried away by this wind of optimism. He wrote: "Holy Scripture may be taught in a joyous and playful way," and—still more surprising from his pen—"A man unable to laugh aloud has no right to call himself a Christian." This benevolent and merry disposition would not last long.

When Calvin returned from his exile in Strasbourg, at the request of the crestfallen Genevan citizens, he made up for everything by wielding an iron fist. Whoever was not behind him unconditionally was against him and must be laid low.

He condemned the playing-cards manufacturer, Pierre Ameau (a wealthy and respected citizen; splendid packs of cards) to walk through Geneva bareheaded, in his shirt, kneeling and pleading for mercy in each public square.

He banished the theologian Castellion, who had claimed that "to stray is not to sin," who opposed Calvin's tragic vision of predestination, and who held that man can be redeemed, right up to the last moment.

He fined Bonnivard, the official chronicler of the city, for drinking and playing dice with the French poet Clément Marot.

He burned the Spanish-born humanist and physician Michael Servetus, who loathed and attacked the concept of the "Holy Trinity" and who might equally well have been burned by Rome. But by doing so, Calvin took many more lives than he thought. Servetus, a great anatomist and stiff ripper, had discovered the lesser circulation of the blood (that is, between the heart and the lungs). His execution in Geneva delayed the publication of his work until the eighteenth century. But God is with us: Harvey rediscovered the whole thing about seventy years later.

Now Geneva, like the Catholic Inquisition, had its executioners, its heretics, its stakes, its religious terrorism: a "liberal" disaster. But we should be reminded that Calvin had no time for *amoenitates*. He was the despotic master of a tiny, fighting city, a "New Jerusalem" for some, a "cesspool of paganism, subversion, and iniquity" for others. A painful thorn in the flesh of the Vatican, a "scandal city" of about twelve thousand inhabitants that every Catholic power wanted to crush and destroy.

The truth is that Geneva was a formidable war-machine. Thirty printers, most of them of French origin, worked night and day to flood Europe with anti-Papist pamphlets. They worked well. And after the public dedication, in June 1559, of his academy (now the University of Geneva)—the only institution, along with the academy of Lausanne, capable of training ministers, missionaries, and martyrs of the new faith in the French language—Calvin wrote to his French friends: "Send me raw wood" (by which he meant students) "and I

will give you back arrows." Those arrows eventually reached the four
corners of Europe and flew as far as Brazil and Florida, to the rage
and dismay of the Catholic states.

On December 12, 1602, one of the longest nights of the year,
thirty-eight years after Calvin's death, Geneva was attacked without
warning by a strong party of the Duke of Savoy, equipped with long,
specially constructed ladders and bombs designed to blast open the
drawbridge and the city gates. Luckily, the night assault was re-
pelled. The next morning the walls were decorated with the heads of
slain enemy soldiers and that evening Bernese troops, arriving at full
speed from Lausanne, entered the city to the cheers of the population. But everything was over. The heroic period was over. Until the
French invasion of 1798, the tiny Republic of Geneva led a relatively
peaceful life.

✦ ✦ ✦

With the exception of the magnificent French prose of Calvin's *Institution de la religion chrétienne*, published in Basel by Thomas Plat-
ter, and—a little later—the *Psaulmes du Roi David*, translated by
Théodore de Bèze and "rhymed" by Clement Marot, both works of
Frenchmen, sixteenth-century Geneva had very little to contribute
to the fine arts or the literature of the time. It is no wonder: a city
where pleasures and distractions as innocent as backgammon were
banned, where the erotic force in Marguerite de Navarre, Rabelais,
Ronsard, and Brantôme was absolutely taboo, where a sentence or a
curse was sufficient to bring you to the gallows, did not encourage
exuberance and fantasy in the fine arts and literature.

What remained is the unique and striking example of a grim,
hard-working, and very strong theocracy ruled by a despotic master,
and living willy-nilly "under the yoke of Jesus Christ." No doubt the
Calvinist experience, along with the *bise noire* (Geneva's icy north
wind), has given a darker cast to the Genevan character and endowed
it with strength and endurance. No doubt it shaped a moralistic and
puritan society (fostering also the hypocrisy that naturally accompa-

nies moral rigor and puritanism), which, for a time at least, was closer to Sparta than to Athens—a city of pedagogues, scientists, and introverts.

Almost two centuries later, Voltaire, who had settled at Ferney, a stone's throw from the Genevan border, made fun of this Genevan cultural void:

> Pour tout plaisir Genève psalmodie
> Du roi David les antiques concerts
> Croyant que Dieu se plaît aux mauvais vers.

[By way of pleasure, Geneva intones the hackneyed Psalms of King David, in the belief that God enjoys bad poetry]

Let us now drift on to the gentler, more amiable waters of the seventeenth and eighteenth centuries.

✦ ✦ ✦

Théodore de Bèze, Calvin's successor at the head of theocratic Geneva was a much milder mentor—a worldly Frenchman adopted by the Genevans, a former secretary of Prince Antoine de Bourbon, the author in his youth of love poems that would make decent girls blush, an outstanding Latinist who exchanged letters with the best minds of Switzerland and Europe. His chief concern was to develop the academy, and he does so with tremendous success. If you look at the matriculation register of noble students, "Stenmata and Emblemata," you will see that the flower of the European aristocracy went through Geneva for short or longer stays in the course of a *Kavalierreise* or a *Bildungsreise*.

This said, the seventeenth century was, until the Revocation of the Edict of Nantes, an uneventful century. Calvin's menacing shadow receded. Theocracy and theology, a bit numb in their joints, took a long-deserved nap. It is noteworthy that, long before the Revocation, Geneva welcomed foreigners of diverse origins and conditions and assimilated them with surprising speed. The city was ready for the onrush of 1684, when French refugees entered the "New Jerusalem" by the thousands, sometimes with the money they were able to save, always with their professional skills in banking, watchmaking, textiles, or silk fabrics, bringing added value to the community.

At the end of the century, throughout Protestant Switzerland, the theologians reawakened from their slumbers. Their names were Turretini for Geneva and Werenfels for Basel. You can see their portraits hanging in university libraries: portly gentlemen with rosy cheeks, powdered wigs, and a twinkle in their eyes. They are almost forgotten today and should not be. For they were highly cultivated men, not only of faith but, following Montaigne's requirement, of "good faith," friends of Bayle or Fontenelle, confirmed Copernicans, readers of Swift, praisers of Descartes and Newton. Their motto was *Tolerantia, caritas, pax, sanctitas*. They were the founders of an "enlightened Protestantism" and, above all, the men who established a long-lasting truce between science and religion by totally and radically separating the two. The revelations of faith and the observations of science now belong to different worlds. Science is not expected to follow religion, nor religion to control science. There is no overlap, and thus total freedom. For this reason, in Switzerland scientific observation was not linked, as it was in the family of the French Encyclopaedists, with religious skepticism. Mathematicians and astronomers, like the Eulers in Basel, naturalists or botanists, like Albrecht Haller in Bern or Sénebier and Etienne Dumont in Geneva, were also convinced and declared Christians, as well as entirely free researchers. This clear-cut attitude would become of great significance and benefit for Geneva.

Obviously, Geneva could not be like Venice or, later, Vienna—a city of uncontrolled passions or romantic love. Venus was killed in Geneva by Calvinistic misogyny and, later, Victorian prudery. Passion was reserved for illustrious visitors such as Byron, Balzac, Shelley, or Liszt. In fact it was expected of them: the gallery would have been disappointed if they had behaved too properly.

Geneva could not be, like Florence, a place of artistic and sensuous delight. Aesthetic boldness was stifled by moralism and its corollary, "introspection." That is why Geneva does not have the splendid, erotic, flying bodies of Füssli, but the cruel and pitiful subhumans, suffocating with self-importance and stupidity, of Rodolphe Toepffer's cartoons.

But Geneva could obviously be—and was for a while—the European capital of the natural sciences, since there is nothing ethically, morally, or sexually wrong in dealing with fossils, pollen, orchids, or beetles. A passion for bugs does not drive one to hell. On top of that, since the time of Haller and Rousseau, Swiss of all conditions have been nuts about nature. Love of nature instead of erotic love? Who can say?

✦ ✦ ✦

As a result, any serious scientific (though not any political) theory could be explained and taught freely in eighteenth- and nineteenth-century Geneva: a boost to the development of experimental psychology, parapsychology, pediatry, and palaeontology.

The first copy of Darwin's *Origins of Species* to reach the continent landed on the desk of the eminent Genevan botanist Alphonse de Candolle. Darwinian evolution was immediately introduced and expounded at Geneva University by the palaeontologist Carl Vogt (a political refugee from Germany after the failure of the 1848 Revolution) who boldly stated, with the amused blessing of Auguste Bouvier, then moderator of the Company of Ministers and head of the Genevan Church, that it was better to be "a perfected ape than a degenerate Adam." This is all the more astonishing as teaching of the Darwinian theory of evolution was forbidden in several American states as late as World War II.

Even more important, there is a botanical library in Geneva that is second only (in pre-Linnaean works) to the library at Kew Gardens in London. More important still, since the late seventeenth century, Genevan botanists, in constant contact with Dutch or British navigators or colleagues who provided them with seeds, roots, bulbs, rhizomes, and the like, have transformed the tiny territory of Geneva into a kind of garden of Eden, a botanical dream. Rare trees may pop up anywhere at random. I have one on my own little estate: *plaqueminia japonica*. It is a mean-looking tree, about fifty feet tall, that drops white, foul-smelling berries in springtime. As there is no such tree within a radius of two hundred miles, a Japanese expert gives me a ring from the Botanic Garden every other year or so and comes by to take a look. I am no exception. In Geneva, this happens all the time, and may happen to almost anybody.

When I am told by my foreign friends that Genevans are sullen, gruff in manner, standoffish, and inhospitable, I can always retort: "Okay, but we have so many foreign trees."

✦ ✦ ✦

How, really, did it come about? Who paid for the microscopes, the laboratories, the ant colonies "in vitro," the aquariums for the study of amoebae and different varieties of sea weed? Who paid for all that gardening?

The answer is the Genevan bankers. All, or almost all, of the botanists, biologists, geologists, and entomologists whose names adorn the streets surrounding the university came from bankers' families. They were, and still are, fabulously well-to-do.

What kind of banks? Family banks of Protestant patricians. Max Weber and Herbert Lüthy have explained at some length the mechanism linking Protestantism and capitalism. It is a brilliant demonstration. I will not go back over it. All I can say is that the Revocation of the Edict of Nantes was the biggest blunder Louis XIV ever made, and he made many.

He drove out hundreds of thousands of able men and women, craftsmen, men of learning, businessmen, jurists, and the like, who spread all over the planet like so many drops of quicksilver. These drops soon reassembled and built up the best banking and trading network in the world, based on a common faith, family ties, a high measure of trust, a minimum of paper work, and a degree of discretion that frustrated the prying curiosity of all kinds of *Contrôleurs des finances* and tax officers.

Louis XIV really gave the Protestants their chance. They—and Geneva—took it. Genevan bankers and traders smuggled into France products that were barred by French customs, such as *indienne* cotton fabrics woven and printed in huge quantities in Geneva. They may also have been indirectly engaged in the trade in black slaves, because ships sailing to the cotton states would carry slaves from West Africa and cotton on the way back to Europe. They made considerable profits, probably on both routes.

✦ ✦ ✦

I once heard the late historian of religions, Joseph Campbell, describe the traditional pattern of a Navajo family in the early 1950s as father, mother, one child, and one white student of anthropology.

Similarly, the ideal pattern of a Genevan banker's family would have been: one banker or trader with correspondents and stringers all over the world; one member of the city's *Petit conseil*, or governing executive, which was still reserved to prominent citizens; one minister of the church; one research scientist, often a very good one, working and publishing on such matters as the bones of mammoths, the structure of crystals, the acclimatization of New Zealand sheep in Switzerland, and so on; one or two extremely well educated daughters, without any "Cinderella complex," fluent in Latin, English, and history, who would marry either in the same milieu, in order to make the family's fortress even more impregnable, or in Berlin, Amsterdam, St. Petersburg, or New York, in order to improve the efficiency of the network.

One good point in the Calvinist morality, which is frustrating in so many other respects, is that from the beginning it paid close attention to the education of girls. They were not disregarded: they were expected to learn as much and as quickly as boys.

Has this ideal pattern changed much since the eighteenth and nineteenth centuries? It is customary in Geneva to make jokes about the stinginess and parsimony of the Genevan bankers. There may be something in that. But I suspect they may have spread those jokes themselves as a kind of decoy. In fact, some of the bankers were so good that we exported them. Necker, Louis XVI's finance minister and the father of Madame de Staël was a Genevan banker. The Gallatin Bank, attacked by Jesse James in American folk songs, and the preferred prey of many other outlaws besides, was a Genevan bank.

Some of the bankers were even lavishly generous and, since it was not easy to be a Maecenas in a city where art production was not abundant, they became philanthropists. They founded clubs or societies against prostitution or, like Jean-Jacques de Selon, against the death penalty. They were philosemites, philoarmenians or, like Jean-Gabriel Eynard, philhellenes.

Jean-Gabriel Eynard was at once an outstanding and a typical figure of nineteenth-century Geneva. He was a young diplomat at the Congress of Vienna in 1815, at which the present boundaries of Switzerland and of Geneva were traced and at which the "Genevan lobby" received unconditional help and support from the Corfiot Count Capo d'Istria, then a counselor at the Russian Court. Subsequently Eynard made a huge fortune as finance minister of the Grand Duchy of Tuscany and, later on, in the wheat trade at Genoa.

When the Greek War of Independence against Turkey broke out, Eynard started to repay his debt to the Greek Capo d'Istra. He organized a volunteer corps that joined the freedom fighters and he armed it at his own expense.

After the savage massacre of Chios, which inspired the painter Delacroix, the survivors, mostly women and children, were sold as slaves to the Turks on the marketplace of Prevesa in Epirus. Eynard sent emissaries to Prevesa with orders to buy back these Greek captives by the hundreds—and this was done.

He paid for half the ships of the British naval squadron that sunk the Turkish fleet at the Battle of Navarino. For years, after Greek independence, he covered the deficit of the Bank of Hellas, which was new and, as one might expect, poorly managed. When he died in Geneva in 1863, it was a national day of mourning throughout Greece. A beautiful portrait was made of Eynard in the year of his death by the Genevan photographer Henri-Antoine Boissonnas: it shows a large, benevolent face, under bushy eyebrows, and an expression full of intelligent compassion and wit.

✦ ✦ ✦

"Nostalgia" is a word coined in the late seventeenth century by the Austrian physician Andreas Hofer (no connection with the Tyrolean freedom fighter of Weber's *Der Freischütz*) to describe the typical homesickness of Swiss mercenaries fighting under foreign flags. Nostalgia for childhood as a paradise lost is the most recurrent topic in the literature of French-speaking Switzerland. Read J.-J. Rousseau, read Toepffer, H. F. Amiel, read Guy de Pourtalès. It is a haunting note, as if adulthood was the age of lead, the passport to sin and perdition.

Since the sixteenth century, pedagogy has been not only a Genevan but a Swiss mania. The raised index finger of the pedagogue, frequently represented in pre-Romantic and Romantic silhouetted papercuts, could well be the logo of nineteenth-century Switzerland.

After the publication of Rousseau's *Emile* (1762), Whig members of the British Parliament began to send their sons to school in Geneva, then still an independent Republic. After saving the orphans, hoodlums, and dropouts of central Switzerland from hunger in the great famine of 1816–1817 and educating them by revolutionary methods to the point where he succeeded in turning them into decent and useful citizens—much to the dismay of the aristocrats—the Swiss teacher and philanthropist Jean-Henri Pestalozzi gained European renown and Switzerland became, in foreign eyes, a kind of pedagogic utopia.

Private schools bloomed in Geneva. Rodolphe Toepffer, the most ferocious cartoonist of the nineteenth century (Daumier and Wilhelm Busch are mild in comparison), had a boarding school in Geneva; students from all over Europe flocked to it. Toepffer, a worshiper of walking like his forerunner, J.-J. Rousseau, used to take them for weeks of trekking in the Swiss Alps.

Not only did French Switzerland attract students by the hundreds, it also sent teachers abroad. It was the beginning of a chosen, often pleasant exile, far less bitter than that of the Swiss soldiers. Lots of preceptors, tutors, and governesses were invited to educate the offspring of patrician and "grand bourgeois" families throughout Europe, but especially in England, Germany, and Russia. The Swiss "nanny" or governess is a familiar character in Victorian and Russian short stories of the late nineteenth century.

After Paracelsus, tutor of a Tartar prince in Samarkand, Admiral Le Fort, mentor and counselor of Peter the Great, and La Harpe, teacher of Czar Alexander II, you will find these preceptors and "nannies" in families such as the Romanoffs, Mountbattens, Hohenzollerns, Tolstois, Bismarcks, Moltkes, and so on. Very often, they are country girls with an excellent upbringing and the unpretentious poise and decency frequently to be found in rural milieux.

Perhaps one of the most engaging of these governesses was Aloyse, a mailman's daughter from Canton Vaud, who was in the imperial Hohenzollern family for years, before World War I. After Wilhelm II abdicated and left for exile in the Netherlands, Aloyse went back to the family farm, laden with imperial gifts and certificates of meritorious conduct, and went quietly insane. She had seen too much of the high life, everything had been too much of a dream for her to return to country life, however pleasant and interesting it may have been in Canton Vaud, where, in the early years of the present century, there were still some farmers who used to read a few verses of the New Testament in Greek before setting out for the fields. Aloyse forgot her own name and wandered helplessly whenever she strayed from home. She was convinced she had been the only real love of the Kaiser, seemingly not a man interested in women (remember the "Phili Eulenburg scandal"). Aloyse was put in an insane asylum where doctors supplied her with rolls of brown wrapping paper and colored chalk, and she spent the rest of her life there, happily drawing gorgeous court dances or mazurkas at Potsdam or Neukönigstein, fireworks displays, Christmas parties teeming with Grand Marshals and Black Hussars in shakos and splendid uniforms. Most of Aloyse's chalk drawings have been saved. They express a strange "slow waltz" kind of happiness, with nothing that suggests a disturbed or tormented mind.

At the turn of this century, in Geneva, Lausanne, Bern, and Zurich, Swiss psychiatrists started giving paper, ink, pencils, and colors to their patients, guessing that if they really had something "else" to say, they might say it that way, which some of them did. At the time, this therapy was uncommon in Europe, where "wild" art was disregarded when not destroyed. Swiss *paidagogia* was once more on a new road. In the city of Lausanne, you will find an interesting *Musée de l'art brut*, where the productions of people "outside the realm of the fine arts," whether inmates of mental asylums or not, are on display. Contrary to most visitors' expectations, the whole collection gives an impression of mad and enthralling mirth. Aloyse has an entire room to herself.

The tradition of Swiss nomadic teachers was kept alive until the later forties. My grandfather was "lecteur de français" at the court of Weimar in his youth; my father was the tutor of Titulesco's children in Romania before World War II; my sister was in Anthony Eden's family just after World War II; and we are by no means exceptional.

✦ ✦ ✦

After the radical revolution of 1846 Rousseau came back into fashion in Geneva. Research into education was a major concern of conservative patricians as well as progressive radicals. The first European laboratory of experimental psychology and parapsychology was established by Flournoy at Geneva University in 1891. Flournoy was intensely interested in mediumistic phenomena, and his book *Des Indes à la planète Mars* (*From India to the Planet Mars*), a study of the visions of the medium Hélène Smith, which turned up with a graphically superb Martian alphabet, sold more than one hundred thousand copies and was translated into more than ten languages. It was the biggest Genevan hit on the book market since *La Nouvelle Héloïse*.

Thus, when the *Institut Jean-Jacques Rousseau*, alias *Institut des sciences de l'éducation* was inaugurated in 1912 (the bicentenary of Rousseau's birth), it was the result of a long and rich tradition. Before becoming director, for more than thirty years, of this now world-famous institution, the pedagogue and psychologist Jean Piaget published in the Institute's periodical his earliest reflections on the structures of intelligence in the child.

Perhaps Geneva's most important contribution to European and world culture in the nineteenth century was the foundation in 1864 of the International Red Cross Society. Henry Dunant, who launched the Red Cross idea, was raised in the turmoil of the radical revolution of 1846 and in the thick of a religious quarrel between supporters of the pietist "Great Awakening," a revivalist movement, and the regular Calvinist church of Geneva. Strongly influenced by the "Awakening," Dunant was a high-strung, mystical, unbalanced character but, once convinced that God was on his side, he could be astonishingly efficient. At the age of twenty or so, with a handful of Genevan and French friends, he had already founded the *Union chrétienne des jeunes gens*, better known in the States as the YMCA.

Like so many other useful things, the idea of the Red Cross was in fact a product of sheer luck. In the year 1859, as the Italo-Franco-Austrian war broke out in Italy, Dunant was the unhappy administrator of a Genevan wheat-milling company in Mons Djemila, Algeria. He had already made himself fairly unpopular among the French settlers by writing prophetic pamphlets denouncing the evil deeds of colonialism. They refused to sell him the land that he needed and was ready to pay for. They considered him an oddball. So, it was to obtain the support of Napoleon III for the affairs of his company that Dunant, in a hired tilbury, followed the French army to Italy. He reached the little Italian town of Castiglione one day after the Franco-Italian victory of Solferino, named after the neighboring village, on June 25, 1859. The battle had been a real butchery: forty thousand dead, to say nothing of the wounded. The French *Service de santé aux armées* was scandalously ill equipped, its few ambulance drivers panicky and overworked. Through negligence, the entire stock of medicines and compresses had remained stranded in the port of Genoa. And we should not forget that under the conscription system, the life of an ordinary soldier was rated cheaper than that of a horse. There were three veterinary surgeons for ten thousand horses and one military surgeon for the same number of men. The sight of the battlefield was appalling. In Castiglione, Dunant mobilized the whole of the civilian population, turned the church into a lazaretto, and organized first aid for the wounded without distinction of friend and foe, and with amazing authority and efficiency.

Two years later, in a fit of mystical exaltation, Dunant wrote, or rather virtually dictated from inspiration, his famed *Un Souvenir de Solférino*, an unbearably realistic and cruel description of a battle he had not seen. This short and violent book shattered the European intelligentsia and won Henry Dunant applause from Victor Hugo, Zola, the Goncourts, George Sand, and several crowned heads. In a few months he had gained European fame and prepared the ground for his humanitarian dream. This dream was soon to become reality. With the aid of such prominent Genevan citizens as General Guillaume-Henri Dufour, the savior of the Confederation during the Swiss Secessionist War of 1848, and the military surgeon Louis Appia, another Genevan witness of the Battle of Solferino, Dunant composed the statutes of the First Geneva Convention on the Treatment of Wounded Soldiers. In the year 1864, an international conference was held in Geneva, and the Geneva Convention was signed by fourteen major European powers, much against the wishes of their respective chiefs-of-staff, who feared that the presence of neutral observers and sanitarians on the battlefield might be a nuisance. In those days of triumph for this entirely Genevan enterprise, Dunant—who had fathered it—was, much to the surprise of the foreign plenipotentiaries, virtually absent from the feast. In the meantime, he had caused and suffered a minor financial disaster. He was bankrupt and had therefore been downgraded to the modest condition of recorder of the conference. Brooding on his destiny, half-hidden behind a huge Corinthian pillar, he wrote down every word uttered in his fine, slightly feminine handwriting.

As I compose these lines, more than three hundred Swiss or Genevan field officers from the International Red Cross are in Kuwait, Baghdad, Amman, and Riyadh, to deal with the needs and arrange for the exchange of tens of thousands of prisoners of war.

2. "Genève, ville internationale"

ZURICH

Gordon A. Craig

3. Merchant port of Zurich, 1812

THE FIRST TIME that I went to Zurich was in November 1983 when I was beginning work on my book about the city. It was a dark, cold season—not the right weather for seeing Zurich for the first time—but my mind was not, in any case, bent upon tourist attractions. I lived in a motel on the Universitätsstrasse that catered to a lively international clientele, a good proportion of whom were Iranians who had fled the revolution in their own land and were awaiting visas that would permit them to go to the United States. The hubbub that attended their discussion of the frustrations and *longueurs* of this process made it seem advisable to me to spend as little time as possible in their company, so I arose early and after breakfast went directly to that marvelous refuge, the *Zentralbibliothek*, where I passed under the approving eyes of Salomon Gessner and Johann Jakob Bodmer and the book-laden cherub who sit in stone above the portal and made my way to the reading room, where I remained for the next nine or ten hours.

The *Lesesaal* is a rectangular chamber, with a skylight and five long tables, each with twenty-eight places. It is bare of decoration, except for some large plaster ornamentation around the edges of the skylight and the pillared wooden railing, probably oak, that rims the narrow balcony on either side. And except, of course, for the books— *Helvetica* in the balcony, *Rechtswissenschaft* below—but these have been uniformly and rather unimaginatively bound, and the result is not aesthetically exciting. The total effect, however, is one of sober comfort, not dissimilar to that of the city itself, and it is conducive to work, and work I did, alternating between the infinite riches in the balcony and the ancient copies of the *Neue Zürcher Zeitung* and the *Eidgenössische Zeitung* that were piled at my seat below.

It is difficult, of course, to sit at a desk for ten hours without interruption, and so, in the course of the working day, I made short sallies into the streets and soon discovered that a great deal of Zurich history lay around me within a very short compass. I made a practice at midday of walking down to the Limmat, where I used to lunch on the Rathaus bridge on sausages and fruit and chocolate bought from the stalls, after which I would wander about in the neighborhood for half an hour. One day, at the other end of the bridge, I discovered a plaque on the side of a building that said that this was the former location of the Hotel Red Sword and that Mme. de Staël, Tsar Alexander I, Emperor Joseph II, August Wilhelm Schlegel, Johann Gottlieb Fichte, Alexandre Dumas, Johann Wolfgang Goethe, Marshal Ney, Ludwig Uhland, General Doumouriez, and the composers Mozart, Brahms and Carl Maria von Weber had all been guests there, presumably not at the same time. Another time I ventured a little further and walked up the Schlüsselgasse on the left bank of the stream to the courtyard of St. Peter's Church, where the grave of the eighteenth-century pastor and physiognomist Johann Caspar Lavater is located and, opposite the church, the house in which Goethe and the Grand Duke Carl August of Saxe-Weimar visited him in November 1780, an occasion that the poet described as "the seal and the highest peak of our journey.[1] And a little bit further up the hill, I found the grove of lindens where the Romans had a customs house and where they killed the Christians Felix and Regula, who, we are told, as soon as they were beheaded, tucked their severed heads underneath their arms and made their way across the Limmat to where the Water Church now stands, where they were buried and became the patron saints of the city.

Not far from the *Zentralbibliothek* on the right side of the Limmat, running uphill from the river level, is the Spiegelgasse, where Gottfried Keller, Zurich's greatest literary figure, attended the School for the Poor. Here the Hessian refugee Georg Büchner, the author of *Woyzek* and the *Death of Danton*, lived in 1836 and 1837 when he was a lecturer on comparative anatomy at the university, and here—actually in the house next door to Büchner's—lived another more unconditional subverter of the bourgeois order, Vladimir

Ilyitch Lenin, in the last years before he went off to the Finland Station. Not far away—one might almost think that the neighborhood had the power of attracting free spirits—there was once, at the juncture of the Spiegelgasse and the Niederdorfstrasse, a Cabaret Voltaire, where Tristan Tzara and his friends held forth, and the Dada movement was born, and close by, in the surviving Guildhouse Zur Meise, Tzara read his first manifesto, on July 23, 1918, and declared, "Here in the paunchy soil [of Zurich] we cast our anchor!", an announcement that elicited shock and indignation from the city's conservative *Bürgertum*.[2]

A little further along the Limmat Quai towards the lake stands the cathedral, the Grossmünster, and here in the crypt one can find the sculpted figure of Charlemagne, with orb and sword and crown, which used for many years to stand on the cathedral's tower, watching over the city, as Keller describes it in the first edition of *Green Henry*. Around the corner is the Kirchgasse and, halfway up its cobbled course, the office of the great Reformer Huldrych Zwingli, when he was the cathedral's pastor, and the place from which he went to meet his death in the war against the Catholic cantons that ended in defeat at Kappel in October 1531. And a little further on, where the Kirchgasse meets the Hirschgraben, one finds the Stone House in which the Ritter Manesse, the collectors of the songs of the Minnesänger, lived in the thirteenth century.

So much history in such a little room, and yet today so dominated and almost overwhelmed by the modern city of wealth and luxury, whose boutiques and *couturiers'* shops and smart restaurants crowd in along the lane where Zwingli walked and the base of the hill where the Romans once collected tolls, whose *grands magasins*—Jelmoli, Bally *e tutti quanti*—jostle against *hotels de luxe* and discreet but internationally known banking houses along the Bahnhofstrasse, whose circumference is lined with corporate headquarters, and whose hills, the Adlisberg and the Zürichberg, are filled with the mansions of the children of high degree.

The Bahnhofstrasse is a foreshortened version of Fifth Avenue or the Kürfürstendamm or the Rue de Rivoli, and like them without strong local or national character. Walking along it one afternoon, I encountered, in the neighborhood of the Paradeplatz, almost completely surrounded by banks, a man wearing lederhosen and playing an *Alpenhorn*. I could not decide whether he was doing so for the entertainment of the bankers (who were presumably busily at work providing a safe refuge for the funds of people who did not want others to know how much money they had or where it came from) or in an effort to encourage pedestrians to return to ancient Swiss virtue and simplicity. If the latter, he was clearly having no effect, for they were not to be diverted from the materialistic enticements that filled the windows of every shop or boutique that they passed.

Modern Zurich is not a place in which those of small means are comfortable. In his memoirs, Arthur Koestler, who came to the city in 1935 from Nazi Germany via Paris, wrote:

> We found it more difficult to be poor in Zürich than in Paris. Although Zürich is the largest city in Switzerland, it has an intensely provincial atmosphere, saturated with opulence and virtue. On Montparnasse one could regard poverty as a joke, as the extravagance of bohemians; but Zürich had neither a Montparnasse, nor inexpensive bistros, nor that kind of humor. In this clean, philistine, orderly city, poverty was simply degrading; and, if we were no longer hungry, we were nevertheless very poor.[3]

Fifty-eight years later, one can understand Koestler's feelings. Zurich today is so redolent of money that it has been said that gold gives a certain coolness and suspicion to the atmosphere and that, with all their friendliness, Zurichers have, so to speak, a little hard line around the mouth.

Five years ago, the novelist Rolf Schneider wrote an article in which he called Zurich "the schizoid city," going on to say that there was something undecided, bipolar, even neurotic about its inhabitants, and about the city itself, which "mirrors this plainly in its appearance." "Strangely enough," he wrote, "the city's river, the

Limmat, does not flow into the lake, but out of it. It dominates the middle of the town then to a degree that leads to such a radical bifurcation that there is no real architectural center, so that the river itself is the center, that is, just water, a swift, heedlessly onrushing stream. The city hall itself, a beautiful building, stands on a bridge in the middle of the Limmat, and the water runs beneath it and goes on."[4]

Schneider's bold attribution of a split personality to the city is suggestive. For surely modern Zurich is sundered from parts of itself, from history, for example, which goes all but unnoticed by the hordes of visitors from abroad, a state of ignorance that the city fathers, who know the value of tourism and are adept in ways to nurture it, find it expedient not to try to correct. And there are other, more grievous divisions in this beautiful city. Although it is rightly proud of the recognition and the financial support that it gives to young writers and artists and musicians, it is separated from the more avant-garde sections of the cultural community, who are always complaining that they can expect no support for anything that is too modern or seems in any way to be revolutionary. The case of Dada has already been mentioned. The history of the Zurich theater since the Second World War is another case in point. In 1969, Max Frisch wrote an article about the dismissal of the directors of the Zurich *Schauspielhaus* after three months in office in which he pointed out that the reason given was that the plays they chose followed a constant and monotonous social-critical line. The city's leading newspapers argued that the directors had violated the traditions of "our *Schauspielhaus*." Frisch pointed out that, during the war years, when Zurich had a truly distinguished theater, the same newspapers denigrated it as "a émigré-Jewish-Marxist theater." They recognized it as "our *Schauspielhaus*" only after the war, as it became steadily weaker.[5]

Finally, modern Zurich is divided from its own younger generation. The beginning of the 1980s saw a virtual rebellion of youth in Zurich, and one that was not a protest against war and rearmament or destruction of the environment and exploitation of the Third

World but rather an uprising against the culture of the Bahnhof-strasse, the stifling materialism, and the pressures to conform. In the riots that began on May 30, 1980—touched off by the city's decision to grant 61 million Swiss francs for the renovation of the Opera House while balking at building a youth center that would give young people an inexpensive place to go in the evenings—the demonstrators carried placards reading, "We are your cultural corpses" and "We have reason enough to weep without your tear-gas." They talked about the "polar ice" that encompassed them and turned their lives into an arctic wasteland. Their goal was modest but distinctly utopian: they wanted a youth center, but they wanted it to be autonomous, that is, free from any government control.[6]

Official Zurich was largely uncomprehending, and the conservative press fastened upon the kind of excesses that accompany such movements to argue that the complaints of the youth were unjustified. A youth center was built, but then was attacked as a center of drugs and anarchy and—because of its claim of autonomy—as being against the law, and in March 1982 it was finally bulldozed to the ground by the police on the orders of the City Magistracy. The result was a profound alienation between generations, a not inconsiderable rise in the suicide rate among young people, and an increase in drug use that soon made a needle park out of the elegant Platzspitz at the confluence of the Limmat and the Sihl, which was James Joyce's favorite square in Zurich and is mentioned in *Finnegans Wake*.[7] When I arrived in Zurich in 1983, the youth movement was dead, and things had quieted down, but I noticed that wherever I went, scrawled in paint on monuments and bridges over the Limmat and the walls of public buildings, the word *Hilflos!* [Hopeless!], a bitter commentary upon the riven state of the communal psyche.

It is perhaps not surprising that, when the time arrived to celebrate the seven hundredth anniversary of the founding of the Swiss *Eidgenossenschaft*, people in all parts of Switzerland, in their concern over the present moral state of their communities, should have begun to think of history as a source of inspiration and revival. This was certainly true of Zurich where the persons most prominent in appealing to the past—writers like Max Frisch and Adolf Muschg, both Zurichers by birth and long residence—were wholly specific about what historical past they meant. They were not seeking to save Zurich, and Switzerland as a whole, from the prevailing materialism by arguing for a return to the rustic simplicity of the early *Eidgenossen*. Frisch had, after all, made it all too clear in his writing that the myth of Wilhelm Tell as usually taught needed considerable correction before it could have any modern utility.[8] They rarely invoked the spirit of Huldrych Zwingli, for with all his virtues the great Reformer suffered from faults that are all too prevalent in the Zurich society today: a decided intolerance for the views of those who did not agree with him, for example, although he did not carry this as far as Luther and Calvin, and a tendency to believe that the accumulation of wealth was in itself a sign of God's grace. Nor did they show much interest in the Enlightenment of the eighteenth century, whose leading figures in Zurich, like Johann Jakob Bodmer, attracted European attention for a while and did much to promote artistic and literary excellence at home, but were always uncomfortable in the presence of real genius, so that the visits of Klopstock and Goethe to the city ended with their hosts wishing that they would go away. The treatment accorded to Lavater and Pestalozzi and the painter Heinrich Füssli showed that the Enlightenment in Zurich was marked by a degree of provincialism that cannot be expected to inspire today's critics of Swiss culture.

Indeed, when such critics looked to the past, they turned their eyes to the years from 1830 to 1860, a time when the political and cultural stagnation that had prevailed in Switzerland since the Congress of Vienna was broken by the electrifying effect of the July Revolution in Paris, so that there were from one end of the country to the other tumultuous assemblies calling for reform and new liberties and within a year eleven cantons, with Zurich in the van, had adopted liberal constitutions.[9]

That these were not democratic constitutions goes without saying.

As in France during the July Monarchy, as in England after the Great Reform Bill of 1832, there was a widening of the franchise to give power to what Richard Cobden once called "the intelligent middle and industrious classes." But men like Paul Usteri and Friedrich Keller, who came to the fore in Zurich in 1830, did not believe that the middle class should be allowed to govern in its own interest, and the merchants and bankers who formed so important a part of their following were the kind of people who still derived as much edification from Adam Smith's *Theory of Moral Sentiments* as they did from his *Wealth of Nations* and instinctively rejected any notion that the pursuit of wealth was an end in itself. The greatest entrepreneur of his generation, the railroad tycoon and banker Alfred Escher, illustrated, in his political career, his active support of Zurich's universities and schools, and through his private benevolence how pervasive civic conscience was among the city's *Bürgertum*. Like the Frenchman Sièyes, who had said that the Third Estate was the nation, the liberals were convinced that the reforms they demanded were in the interest of all classes and would bring them guarantees of human rights and law and justice and opportunities to improve their material lot.

It is not necessary to rehearse the accomplishments of the Zurich liberals in any detail, but one cannot help being impressed, in retrospect, by their breadth of view, their optimism, and their energy. No task seemed to daunt them, and their declared program, in the years after 1830, called for nothing less than a complete modernization of the cantonal government and the creation of an infrastructure that would support a new, prosperous, and equitable society. That this meant the overhauling of administrative structures that had grown ossified with the passage of time goes without saying. With scant respect for tradition, the liberals shook up the system of local government and established rules for popular participation that proved to have positive and far-reaching effects in civic education, laying the basis indeed for the democratic reforms that were to come in the 1870s. In the field of justice, they wrote new codes of civil and criminal procedure and strove to bring the judicial system into accord with scientific principles. They made a careful inventory of cantonal property, and, in the case of buildings that were not being put to social use, sold them and used the proceeds to support hospitals and schools—a policy that had no equivalent in the liberal programs in post-1830 England and France. They drafted comprehensive tax laws to remove the kind of gross inequities that had existed in the old regime, eliminating indirect taxes that bore heavily on the rural population and introducing direct taxes on property at a uniform rate and upon income at a progressive rate. They contributed to the promotion of economic growth in various effective ways without surrendering themselves to complete a Manchesterianism. In 1832, when there were popular protests and acts of violence by cotton spinners because of the introduction of mechanical spinning machines, the *Neue Zürcher Zeitung* reminded its readers of the misery of the cotton spinners who were "scarcely able, by sixteen hours of daily work, to still their own hunger and that of their wailing children with boiled potatoes and thin milk and to cover their nakedness" and added that "the introduction of the weaving machine [which was just beginning] demands earnest and conscientious discussion, which cannot be satisfied in the interests of only one class or by coldly invoking the word freedom of trade."

Statements like this did not mean that Switzerland was free of the ills of industrialism, and it is of course true that in the years after 1860 the tumultuous economic development that took place in Switzerland—and the growth on the one hand of trusts, monopolies, and cartels and on the other of a large industrial proletariat—caused problems that were similar, though on a smaller scale, to those in other countries in the industrial age. But in the liberal period, the attitude to such problems was at least inspired by a degree of social sympathy that was less pronounced in the century's last years.

Notable among the accomplishments of the liberals of 1830 was their work in the field of education, where their reforms were forty years ahead of anything similar in England and France. Here they

built upon the inspiration of Johann Heinrich Pestalozzi and the
liberals of the Helvetian Republic (1798–1801), like Friedrich Stampfer and Johann Rengger, who had sought to actualize the principles
of that great reformer. Because of the political conditions of that
earlier time and the lack of financial resources to support the reforms
that they proposed, the only thing that was accompanied by the Helvetian Republic in the field of education was a system of school in-
spectors, intended to raise standards of education, particularly in
rural schools. This survived and, as Friedrich Stampfer wrote to Paul
Usteri in 1810, was still working effectively in several Swiss cantons at
that time. The liberals of 1830 improved upon that example by legislation that made school attendance compulsory from the ages of six
to sixteen, with subventions to parents to whom payment of the fees
set by local school boards was a hardship. They also established systems of secondary and higher schools, specialized in ways to train all
parts of the population for future careers in business, technology,
agriculture, and trade, and set up new teachers colleges and seminars
with the purpose of increasing the effectiveness of teaching, The
quality of public schools increased so dramatically as a result of these
reforms that there was a significant decline in the attendance of private schools, and in 1867, when the English poet and school inspector
Matthew Arnold completed an extensive investigation of school systems in France, Italy, Germany, and Switzerland, he reported to the
House of Commons that many of the Swiss schools were the best of
their kind in Europe.

This was particularly true in Zurich, where the quality of higher
education was also of a very high order. In 1831, the liberals, in order
to initiate and maintain the intellectual revival of their city, founded
the first new university to be built on Swiss soil since the establishment of the University of Basel in 1460, amalgamating existing
institutions like the school of theology and the medical and political
institutes and, under the guidance of philologist Johann Caspar von
Orelli, devising a new curriculum and appointing a new faculty.
After the creation of the *Bundestaat* in 1848, it was the hope of Alfred
Escher and other Zurich liberals that their university could be trans-

formed and designated as the national university. This ambition was
blocked by the Swiss National Council, under strong pressure from
the Catholic cantons, but in compensation the council voted to establish a national polytechnical institute in Zurich. This opened its
doors in 1852 and in the course of the years became one of Europe's
most famous technical universities. Today, housed in a building designed by Gottfried Semper, the Eidgenössische Technische Hoch-
schule (ETH) stands side by side with the university on the rampart
formed by Remistrasse and Universitätsstrasse, dominating the
lower town, and together they provide a visual reminder of the liberal
period's legacy to Zurich's intellectual and cultural life.

The vitality of Zurich's liberal culture in the nineteenth century
was enriched by the contributions of many people who were not
natives of the city. In one of his histories of Switzerland, Gustav
Widmer comments that it has always taken considerable effort to
awaken in the heart of the *Schwyzer* sympathy for others, and that
this has been particularly true in the case of foreigners suffering mis-
fortune.[10] To the extent that this observation is true, it may have
been inspired by memories of refugees turned back from the borders
during the Second World War. During the liberal years, however,
the Swiss cantons were known for the welcome that they offered to
fighters for freedom in other lands who were forced to seek refuge
beyond their own borders. The followers of Mazzini who were expelled from their homeland by the Austrians, the Polish patriots of
1831, the barricade fighters from Berlin and Milan and Dresden in
1848–1849, the remnants of the armies that fought for democracy in
Baden in 1849, those who were proscribed by Louis Napoleon's coup
d'état in 1851—people such as Filippo de Boni, Felice Orsini, Georg
Herwegh, Richard Wagner, Gottfried Semper, Karl Schurz, Friedrich Theodor Vischer, Wilhelm Rüstow, Francesco de Sanctis,
Paul Armand Challemel-Lacour, and Marc Dufraisse—all found a
place in Zurich on condition that they did not indulge in foreign
politics, and many remained long enough to make a rich contribution to local culture. Particularly in the years after 1830, the policy of
granting asylum to refugees was not without danger for a small

country situated in the center of a primarily conservative continent. Metternich, who gave his name to the era, detested Switzerland and said in 1836 that it made a practice of harboring adventurers, subversive natures, and "*esprits perdus dans le vague*." But, despite the possibility that the Austrian chancellor might seek to form an international coalition to bring pressure, or worse, to bear upon a land that he considered to be a fomenter of anarchy, the liberals persisted, and Zurich and the other cantons profited from the talents of those whose freedom they protected.

There has been a tendency among historians of the modern period to denigrate the spirit and accomplishments of nineteenth-century liberalism. It is true that in Switzerland, as in England and Germany, its spirit changed as the years passed, as new problems and the increasing polarization of politics and society challenged the relevance of its philosophy, and as it fell prey, as John Stuart Mill in his book *Representative Government* said was the fate of all forms of government, to the dangers of special privilege and legislation intended primarily for the dominant class. When this happened in Switzerland, strong movements of popular protest developed all across the land, and in Zurich the powerful Alfred Escher, the father of the *Wirtschaftswunder* that made Zurich the economic capital of Switzerland, was toppled from office. This was the background of the revolution of the early seventies, which brought a transition to direct democracy, so that the number of Swiss citizens living under systems of representative government declined and by 1880, only one canton, that of Freiburg, still retained unrelieved parliamentary government, that is, the system in which the parliament elects the government and makes the laws. But the fall of liberalism in Switzerland was not as precipitous as that in Germany, where the liberals in effect sold out to militarism and absolutism, nor did liberalism disappear, as it did in countries where the polarization of politics squeezed it out of existence. It remained alive to form the basis of the party of the middle called the Progressive Democratic Party, which was founded in 1894 and is still a powerful factor in Swiss politics.

Moreover, it should be remembered that when liberalism was at its height, in the period between 1830 and 1860, its claim to universality was not only validated by the benefits it brought to society as a whole but by the fact that the liberal parties in the different cantons were able to attract talents from above and below their social nucleus and to retain the support of significant sections of other classes. It is not too much to conclude from this that the characteristic forms of liberal politics on the national and the local levels prepared the way for the introduction of direct democracy.

The greatest achievement of Swiss liberalism, in which the Zurich liberals Alfred Escher and Jonas Furrer played a leading role, was the creation of a new and better union of the cantons. This they accomplished by defeating an attempt at secession by the Catholic cantons in a brief and relatively bloodless war in 1847 and then by providing the restored *Eidgenossenschaft* with an effective constitution and institutions to make it viable.[11] Reflecting upon the fact that Metternich and Guizot and Nicholas of Russia would have liked to intervene in the Sonderbund War and held off only because the British foreign secretary Lord Palmerston stood behind the Swiss liberals, the young Karl Marx and Friedrich Engels wrote:

> The despots and the peoples have understood the significance of the struggle in Switzerland, the struggle of modernity with the feudal past, of democracy with aristocratic and jesuistical baseness, very well. . . . The victory is to the advantage of the popular party in every country in Europe; it was a European victory."[12]

Many Swiss liberals felt the same way. Like the seven upright men in Gottfried Keller's story, they were proud of what they had accomplished in 1848, and they regarded their country as a kind of wave of the future, a model of what Europe might become, a forerunner of a continent that would be a union of free countries. This perhaps explains the tremendous popular enthusiasm for the railroad-building of the liberal years. As late as the mid-forties, when rail systems were developing rapidly in England, France, and Germany, there were no

Swiss railways at all. The liberals, however, had from the beginning
been champions of rail construction, and the vision of Zurich entrepreneurs like Martin Escher-Hess and the financial strategy and ne-
gotiating skills of Alfred Escher finally overcame the obstacles imposed by the other cantonal governments and began the elaboration
of a rail system that was integrated with those beyond the national
frontiers. The excitement that attended the opening of the first link
of this system in August 1847—the line from Zurich to Baden—was
doubtless caused in part by a feeling of exhilaration at being part of
a burgeoning movement of European unity and of hearing the new
music that seemed to fill the air as

> Quer durch Europa von Westen nach Osten
> Rüttert und rattert die Bahnmelodie[13]

> [Right across Europe from the west to the east
> Joggles and rattles the song of the train.]

   Some liberals, indeed, were not content to wait for the process of
European liberation and union to take place of its own accord. In
1848, when revolutions broke out from one end of the continent to
the other, leaders like James Fazy of Geneva, Henri Druey of Waadt,
and Jakob Stämpfli of Bern believed that Switzerland should play a
more positive part in the European fight for freedom, and their more
ardent followers talked of raising a force of 120,000 men to come to
the aid of the revolutionary forces in Germany, Hungary, and Italy.
In some cantons, the majority of opinion was opposed to the traditional policy of neutrality, and Tessin not only sent *Freischaren* into
Lombardy but was one of six cantons that favored concluding an
offensive-defensive alliance with Carlo Alberto of Piedmont during
his war with the Austrians. During the Badenese risings of 1848 and
1849, there were many liberals who believed that volunteers should be
allowed to cross the frontier and fight alongside Hecker and Struve
and Sigel, and the federal government had to seal the border to prevent this. Again, during the Crimean War, when liberal opinion in

all European countries was united against Russian absolutism and when Britain, France, and Piedmont had gone to war, even the *Neue Zürcher Zeitung*, whose line in 1848 had been expressed in an editorial that said "We have of late almost forgotten that we are Swiss and that a people has above all to think of itself," changed its position radically and decided that, since this was a war for civilization, Switzerland should raise a force of twelve to sixteen thousand men to support the allies. The federal government clung to its neutral position, but this time did not try to prevent Swiss nationals from joining the Swiss Legions in Britain and France and, as a result, Ulrich Ochsenbein of Bern actually became a brigadier in the French army. Finally, in 1859, Tessiner were among Garibaldi's red-shirts in the movements to create a new Italy, and Wilhelm Rüstow, a former Prussian officer who had become a resident of Zurich in 1853 and a lecturer on tactics to the federal army, served as chief of staff to Garibaldi in Sicily and Naples; and a year later Rüstow and his Zurich friend Emma Herwegh made an abortive plan with the German socialist Ferdinand Lassalle for the creation of a joint German-Italian-Swiss force under Garibaldi's command that would overthrow absolutism in Austria and Germany.

The feeling that Switzerland was unique and was destined to serve as a model for the regeneration of Europe, and even to participate in that process, waned swiftly in the years after 1860, as economic progress made foreign adventures seem unattractive and dangerous and took the edge off liberal idealism. The Zurich novelist Gottfried Keller had believed that his country was different from others. In his last novel, *Martin Salander*, however, he concluded: "*C'est chez nous comme partout.*" He was referring to the avalanche of gold that had seduced the people of Seldwyla, his fictional Zurich, but what he said was true in other ways as well. As Europe, in the wake of the wars of 1866 and 1870, became more insecure and militaristic, as the waning of the free-trade era ushered in a new era of trade wars and imperialism, as the members of the international community formed alliances against each other and gave themselves over to an uncritical nationalism that often verged on jingoism, Switzerland was not un-affected. In 1871, when German residents in Zurich celebrated the victory over France, there was an ugly outburst of xenophobia in that city that was unprecedented and that persisted in a new and assertive Swiss patriotism. It was perhaps notable that the first fruits of the revision of the federal constitution in 1874 was a military re-form that called for a more centralized army with fewer cantonal restraints upon it. Both of these changes were signs of a separation from Europe; the frontiers now seemed to grow thicker and higher; the insistence upon national unity and neutrality became shriller; and as it did so Switzerland seemed to become less international and more provincial.

All of this had an unfortunate effect upon Swiss culture, and one that in the case of many Zürich intellectuals ended the pride in their country that had—from Pestalozzi to Keller and Albin Zollinger and Meinrad Inglin—formerly inspired them. Out of this grew the anti-nationalism of much of the best of Swiss writing in the modern pe-riod. One thinks of Max Frisch, with his debunking of Swiss my-thologies, his attacks upon Swiss institutions like the army, as in his *Dienstbüchlein*, and upon Swiss provincialism, as in the article in the Basel journal *Achtung*, where he complained:

> The Swiss is beginning to be regarded internationally as a representa-tion of the *nouveau riche*. That is not unjustified. Our richness as a nation has not produced any corresponding achievement. We not only lose our ancestors' way of life; inevitably, we mummify it in festi-vals; Swissness becomes a costume and it is cultivated as such;[14]

and his harking back to an older, greater time, in fact, to 1848. His stern critic of his country's fortunes, Anatol Stiller, says at one point that, thanks to the energy and high ideals of the liberals, Switzerland in the middle of the nineteenth century had a sense of purpose and direction. "In those days," he says, "they had a blueprint. In those days they rejoiced in tomorrow and the day after. In those days they had a historical present."[15] In his last book, Frisch suggested that a

country that needs enemies and a policy of neutrality for self-defini-
tion is a dangerous anachronism.[16]

If Frisch seemed to yearn for a revival of the spirit of 1848, Adolf
Muschg calls for a return to the identification with Europe and the
desire to collaborate in changing it that was characteristic of people
like Fazy and Druey and Ochsenbein and Herwegh and other radical
liberals of that earlier time. Muschg flatly challenges the whole idea
of Swiss neutrality in a Europe that has now been freed from the
danger of East-West confrontation and is moving rapidly toward
integration and unity. Not only would collaboration in the European
movement help Switzerland's economy, but it might help find a way
averting the ecological disaster that is now threatening the Forest
Cantons. But, more important than that, Muschg believes that a
Switzerland that profited so greatly from the refugees that came to it
seeking freedom in the 1840s and 1850s must show its gratitude by
contributing to the movement to make all Europe united and free. In
1848, Muschg has written, Switzerland was

> a model for the continent, which for a while had all the European
> powers against it, but the wind of history in its favor. Today, the
> *Musterländchen*, which has become sated, must learn to have a new
> model, the little Gold-Majesty Switzerland must thoroughly repudi-
> ate its consciousness of being a special case in order to become again
> what it once was—and what it must otherwise become in any case,
> only without a will of its own and the pride that comes from indepen-
> dent action—an integral part of Europe, jointly sharing its hopes,
> jointly responsible for its success. That will require of my much
> blessed country a hard piece of work and the overcoming of a good
> deal of *Angst*, the *Angst* of those who have much property and a high
> degree of security.[17]

How acceptable this prescription will be in Zurich it is not easy
to guess, although there will be many who will say that a Zurich
without the Swiss franc would be unthinkable. It is a question about
which a foreigner would perhaps be well advised to remain silent.

Still, as one who loves Zurich, I cannot forget the polar ice or refrain from thinking that active involvement in the movement toward a European economic, monetary, and political union and in the effort to create a common European foreign and security policy, including some integrated European forces, would be a better course for Zurich and all Switzerland to follow than one of clinging to the values of the Bahnhofstrasse.

NOTES

1. Nicholas Boyle, *Goethe: The Poet and the Age*. Vol. 1, *The Poetry of Desire, 1749–1790* (Oxford: Clarendon Press, 1991), p. 311.

2. Thomas Faerber and Markus Luchsinger, *Joyce in Zürich* (Zurich: Unionsverlag, 1988), pp. 23–25.

3. Arthur Koestler, *The Invisible Writing: An Autobiography* (New York: Macmillan, 1954) p. 277.

4. Rolf Schneider, "Die schizoide Stadt: Zürich—teils behabig, teils aufsässig," *Suddeutsche Zeitung*, April 16–17, 1988, p. 171.

5. Max Frisch, "Rede zum Zürcher Debakel" (1969) in *Schweiz als Heimat? Versuche über 50 Jahre*, ed. Walter Obschlager (Frankfurt: Suhrkamp Verlag, 1990), p. 274.

6. On all this, see Michael Haller, "Das Jugend und das Packeis," in *Merian* 36 (1983): pp. 47ff.

7. See Faerber and Luchsinger, *Joyce in Zürich*, pp. 124–26.

8. See, for instance, Max Frisch, *Wilhelm Tell für die Schule* (Frankfurt: Suhrkamp Verlag, 1971).

9. The account of liberal accomplishments that follows is based on my more extensive and detailed description in *Geld und Geist: Zürich im Zeitalter des Liberalismus, 1830–1869* (Munich: Beck Verlag, 1988) (*The Triumph of Liberalism: Zurich in the Golden Age, 1830–1869* [New York: Charles Scribner's Sons, 1989]). There are occasional repetitions of text.

10. Sigmund Widmer, *Illustrierte Geschichte der Schweiz*, 4th ed. (Munich: C. H. Beck Verlag, 1977), p. 331.

11. On the nature of the conflict, which facilitated reconciliation when hostilities ended, see Joachim Remak, *A Very Civil War: The Swiss Sonderbund War of 1847* (Boulder, Colo.: Westview Press, 1993).

12. *Deutsche Brüsseler Zeitung*, December 30, 1847.

13. Detlev von Lilienkron, "Der Blitzzug" (1908), in *Ausgewählte Werke*, ed. Hans Stern (Hamburg: Holsten Verlag, 1964), p. 284. In Lilienkron's poem, however, the music becomes ominous.

14. Max Frisch, *Stichworte*, ed. (Frankfurt: Suhrkamp Verlag, 1985), pp. 151f.

15. Max Frisch, *Stiller*, (Frankfurt: Suhrkamp verlag, 1963), p. 292.

15. Frisch, *Schweiz als Heimat?* pp. 365ff and passim.

17. Adolf Muschg, *Die Schweiz am Ende. Am Ende die Schweiz: Erinnerungen an mein Land vor 1991* (Frankfurt: Suhrkamp Verlag, 1990), p. 173.

4. Zurich Airport

B A S E L

Lionel Gossman

5. Basel

SINCE ROMAN TIMES there has been a major settlement where the city of Basel stands, at the furthest point of navigation on the Rhine, on the great overland route between Northern and Western Europe and Italy, the North Sea and the Mediterranean. For centuries people here have made a living from the transshipment of goods passing between the Low Countries and Italy, and between France and southern Germany. Even today, Basel is one of the nodal points of the European rail network. It is also an important banking center and the headquarters of three of the leading chemical and pharmaceutical companies in the world—all with major operations in the U.S.: Ciba-Geigy, Sandoz, and Hoffmann-Laroche. These giant firms had their beginnings in synthetic dyeing processes originally developed in the second half of the nineteenth century for the silk-ribbon industry. For about three hundred years, until the very end of the nineteenth century, the manufacture of silk ribbon was the mainstay of the Basel economy.

As late as the mid-1800s, Basel was without question the wealthiest and most populous city in German-speaking Switzerland. Today, it is a prosperous medium-sized town of about two hundred thousand inhabitants—coming up for half a million if you include the metropolitan area (the *regio basiliensis*, as the Baselers, ever good Latinists, call it) which stretches into Germany and France. It has one of the great art museums of the world, as well as many specialized museums and galleries, and the usual complement of cultural institutions of any self-respecting European city: a university, a good municipal repertory theatre and opera (including a chamber opera), a music conservatory, and a fine small orchestra. In addition, it is still the home of several distinguished publishing firms.

Zurich, of course, is now the largest and most influential city in Switzerland, having overtaken Basel in the course of the last century.

It is also more centrally situated in the new federal state that came into existence in 1848, and is in many respects more thoroughly Swiss. For Basel is not only, or even first and foremost, a Swiss city. (Nor, for that matter is Geneva, with which Basel has always had feelings of affinity). "Basel isn't Salzburg, Prague or Vienna," as one of its more recent celebrities, the theologian Karl Barth, once wrote, "Basel is Basel."[1] Only a few years ago, elderly Baselers could still be heard saying they were "going to Switzerland," just as they would say they were going to France or Germany. Basel is above all a European city. It is and always has been intensely particularist and inward looking, geographically and culturally eccentric in relation to its neighbors—not only Germany and France, but Switzerland itself. At the same time, it is also and always has been thoroughly cosmopolitan, geographically and culturally a major European crossroads. France and Germany are a fifteen-minute trolley ride away in the northwestern and northeastern suburbs. Nietzsche often complained of the damp, misty climate of Basel, but it was probably the years he spent teaching at the university there (the only job he ever had) that transformed him from a naively patriotic German into the European that he later insisted he always was. No city in Switzerland has deeper roots in European history.[2]

Basel's golden age was the first half of the sixteenth century when the curiosity and open-mindedness of its silversmiths and makers of fine paper, its printers and engravers, made it one of the great centers of northern humanism and Reformation scholarship, the elective home of learned humanists from many lands, such as Reuchlin and Erasmus, who is buried in the cathedral, of artists such as Hans Holbein, of renowned printer-publishers such as Johannes Froben, the friend of Erasmus and the printer of some of the earliest Bibles and editions of classical texts, and the site of a promising modern university, founded in 1450 with the support of the humanist pope Aeneas Silvius Piccolomini, Pius II—the first and for over three centuries the only university in Switzerland.

It was at the dawn of this golden age, in the year 1501, that Basel, which had long been a free Imperial city, joined the Swiss Confederation. Though it did so reluctantly and without enthusiasm, purely for reasons of self-defense, in fact it gave up very little of its sovereignty, since the Swiss Confederation was not much more in those days than a defensive alliance of quite varied and highly independent cities and rural cantons, with no central government and no permanent capital city or court. With the exception of the brief interlude of the Helvetic Republic (1798–1803), Switzerland was not to have either until a major revision of the constitution in 1848. All the cantons thus continued to enjoy a great measure of autonomy and were, to all intents and purposes, independent states. Right down into the nineteenth century, the state or "fatherland," to the citizens of Basel, meant the city-republic of Basel—SPQB, Senatus Populusque Basiliensis, as the city fathers announced with Roman dignity on all the principal buildings.

Though relatively small, even by the standards of the time—about fifteen thousand to nineteen thousand inhabitants until the rapid expansion of the nineteenth century—Basel was famous from the late fifteenth century on for its wealth and its piety. A sociologist seeking an illustration of the Weberian thesis about religion and the rise of capitalism would not have to look further than the city of Oecolompadius. Basel had gone over to the Reformation early, and because of this it became, like its similarly situated sister city Geneva, a place of refuge for religious dissidents: in Basel's case they came from northern Italy, the Spanish Netherlands, France, and the neighboring German-speaking lands. Characteristically, the Basel government did not welcome poor or indigent refugees. Only those who could show they had capital and skills and would not become a burden to the community were welcomed and admitted to citizenship—for a considerable fee, moreover. Many of the families that were later to make up the so-called patriciate or ruling elite immigrated around this time: the Burckhardts, the Bachofens, the Batti-

ers, the Bernoullis, the De Barys, the La Roches, the Le Grands, the
Passavants, the Paravicinis, the Sarasinis or Sarasins, the Socinis or
Socins, the von der Mühlls. Coming from more advanced and progressive societies than their new homeland, these people were not
only wealthy, they were shrewd, experienced, and well-educated
businessmen and men of the world. It was they who transformed
Basel from a medieval guild city into a go-ahead commercial, banking, and manufacturing center with trading interests throughout the
world.

The Basel merchants bought and sold and speculated on all the
major European markets. In addition, they introduced the then-
advanced putting-out method to the manufacture of silk ribbon and
passementerie. By shifting production from highly regulated and
expensive guild artisans in the city to weavers in the countryside, the
putting-out system allowed the merchants to get round restrictive
guild regulations and to vastly increase productivity while lowering
costs. The city-based merchants were essentially middlemen: they
supplied raw materials and the most advanced looms they could find
to their rural weavers; the weavers delivered the finished products to
the merchant's warehouse in the city and were paid by the piece. By
the mid-seventeenth century, Basel had become the chief center for
the manufacture of silk ribbon in Europe (and ribbon, of course, was
a far more important item of clothing in those days than now), ri-
valed only by Krefeld in northern Germany and Saint-Etienne in
France. In addition, the legendary fortunes amassed by the ribbon
merchants or *Bändelherren*, as they were called, became the basis of
a private banking industry that made Basel the chief source of capital
for neighboring Alsace, Baden, and other parts of Switzerland, including Zurich.[3]

Basel's cultural golden age may have been over by the early seventeenth century, but by staying out of trouble in a terribly troubled
time, the city prospered greatly—in part (as Switzerland has sometimes done) through the misfortunes of its neighbors. As opportunities for investing money were still fairly limited in the preindustrial

age, a good deal of the new wealth was channeled into real estate and works of art. Perhaps that is why there is a long tradition of collecting in Basel. The townhouses of the *Bändelherren* or ribbon lords, which served not only as residences but as warehouses and business premises, were grand and elegant. Often they were built from designs for the *hôtels particuliers* of noblemen in the architecture manuals of celebrated French and German architects. (Thomas Mann's *Buddenbrooks*—the action of which takes place in the Hanseatic port city of Lübeck—provides a vivid picture of the way of life of the free-city merchants of the late eighteenth and nineteenth centuries.) Many of the *Bändelherren* also had stately establishments in the Basel countryside to which they retired in the warm weather, or where they went to enjoy the pleasures of the hunt. All bought paintings to decorate the walls of these grand houses but, in addition, several invested heavily in artworks, became connoisseurs themselves, and built up outstanding collections (Burckhardt, Heussler, Faesch, Bachofen). One such, dating back to the Renaissance, was purchased jointly by the city and the university in 1662 and formed the nucleus of the first civic (as distinct from royal or princely) art collection in Europe. The *Herren* travelled widely on business; most spoke several languages. Some settled in foreign places—in Bordeaux and Le Havre, in Vienna and St. Petersburg, in London and later in New York, and there was a constant coming and going between Basel and these outposts of Basel business enterprise. A good deal of the city's commercial success was due to this diaspora on which the home firms could draw for vital information about market conditions and opportunities.

By the mid-seventeenth century the university was in decline, except for a brilliant school of mathematicians (consisting chiefly of several generations of Bernoullis), who upheld the intellectual reputation of Basel through to the end of the eighteenth century. University appointments were in danger of becoming a sinecure for the sons of the *Herren* who for one reason or another did not go into the family business. Intellectual life went on, however, not as brilliantly as during the Renaissance, but still it went on, in private clubs and improvement societies and at social gatherings. The Enlightenment made major inroads among a practical, commercial people whose activities and aspirations corresponded in large measure to the ideals of the *philosophes*. Isaac Iselin, one of the leading figures of the Enlightenment in Switzerland, and Peter Ochs, the chief architect of the Helvetic Republic, were both Baselers. Even the takeover of the university by the local families had its positive side, since it ensured that the old humanist connection between the practical life and the life of the mind was preserved. Nearly all the great merchant families of Basel could count at least one professor or scholar among their members.

In principle, the government of Basel was quite democratic. With minor exceptions, all male citizens had to be members of one of the fifteen trade guilds on which the government of the city-state rested. In practice, from the seventeenth century on things were not so rosy. In the first place, there was a considerable population of noncitizens, both legals and illegals, as we would say, who did much of the menial work and were rigorously excluded from the guild-controlled crafts and trades. As of the last third of the eighteenth century these people were already a majority (7,400 to 7,000, according to Markus Lutz's *Basel Bürgerbuch* of 1818) and by the middle of the nineteenth century they made up two-thirds of the population of Basel. They had no part, not even formally, in the government of the state. Secondly, the population of the politically dependent rural districts surrounding the city, though not as large as that of Zurich or Bern (again Geneva and Basel seem strikingly similar), accounted for sixty-six percent of the total population of the state, and these "subjects" as they were called, were also virtually unrepresented until the effects of the French Revolution made themselves felt at Basel. Finally, neither the Bürgermeister (the head of state) nor the members of the *Kleiner Rat* or executive council were directly elected by the citizenry or by the guild members. Instead, they were selected by the members of the *Grosser Rat* or Senate, who also selected their own replacements

from among the leaders of the guilds. The latter were likewise selected not by the whole guild membership but by the retired and
retiring guild leaders. As a result, the entire ruling caste tended to be
self-perpetuating. In addition, the so-called *Honoratiorenregiment*—
according to which government service, as it was a duty and privilege
of citizenship, was not remunerated and could not therefore be alien-
ated to a paid bureaucracy—ensured that only the very well-to-do
could afford to play an active part in government. The historian Paul
Burckhardt claims that between 1529 and 1798 only four genuine artisans held significant public office in Basel and none was ever Bürgermeister. Basel, in sum, was a strange mixture. It was a commercial
republic of merchants and tradespeople, with no aristocracy and
no high church hierarchy. (The bishop of Basel had been forced out
of the city in 1529.) Yet it was completely dominated by an elite of
wealthy merchant families closely connected to each other by an in-
tricate web of marriages. Often the term patriciate is used to describe
this elite. That is acceptable usage so long as it is clear that we are not
talking about a closed patriciate, as in Venice. Money could and did
open all doors in Basel. As the radical *Nationalzeitung* noted in an
unfriendly article in 1844 (January 4): "Money is the surrogate at
Basel for talent, diligence, knowledge, honor, virtue; with money it
is possible to settle all one's accounts with one's fellow-man." At the
same time it was a pious place: "das fromme Basel," people called it.
In the late seventeenth and eighteenth centuries, the more modest
artisans were increasingly drawn to pietistic forms of religion, but the
elite too—though by no means untouched by the ideas of the Enlightenment—retained for the most part the religious earnestness
that had brought them to the city in the first place. The church was
not only intimately associated with the state (that was normal in
European countries until fairly recently), it was part of the way of life
of all classes of Basel society. Even in the mid-nineteenth century
when a handsome new building was inaugurated for the city's art and
science collections (designed, incidentally, by Jacob Burckhardt's
brother-in-law, the architect Melchior Berri), opening times were

set at four hours through the week and two hours on Sundays—
"after Church," as the regulations stipulated sternly. During Sunday
church services, it should be added, vehicular traffic was forbidden
and the city gates were kept closed.

Not surprisingly, Basel was a pretty conservative place politically.
But not in the style of traditional land-holding ancien regime aris-
tocracies. In international relations the *Herren* were free-traders.
They might even have seemed relatively "liberal" politically, in the
rather Romantic sense that that implied in Germany in the second
and third decades of the nineteenth century. For they were republi-
cans, and were equally opposed to old-style monarchical absolutism
and to the newer Jacobin and Napoleonic despotisms. Napoleon's
Continental Blockade had run completely counter to their interests,
for instance, and at one point, during the so-called Mediation period
(1803–1814), when Switzerland was virtually a French satellite, seven
of the most prominent citizens had been imprisoned for "smuggling." Some were almost ruined by the *dirigiste* policies of Napoleon, which favored French manufactures and which badly hurt the
fledgling cotton industry in Basel. Others, however, made fortunes
in clandestine trade with England. In the reactionary Europe of the
Carlsbad decrees, Basel admitted so many political refugees from
Germany and Austria that the city came to be thought of by the
Prussian and Austrian governments as a dangerous nest of liberals
and revolutionaries.

The most famous refugee was the distinguished theologian De
Wette, a disciple and friend of Schleiermacher. De Wette had written a letter of condolence to the mother of the idealistic student who
had been condemned to death, in 1819, for the assassination of the
well-known playwright and Czarist informer Kotzebue, expressing
understanding for the young man's motives, even while not condon-
ing the crime itself. For his pains, he was suspended from his position at the University of Berlin. The Basel authorities, who had just
determined to build up the city's university and entire educational

system, and who may well have relished sticking a thorn in the side of a regime for which, as merchants and businessmen, they had no sympathy at all, saw an opportunity and promptly hired the suspended professor. Shortly afterwards they offered positions in the faculties of law and medicine to several other scholars who were being pursued by the Prussian authorities for undefined subversive activities (one of them was Carl Follen, who subsequently emigrated to America and became the first professor of German at Harvard) and they steadfastly refused to comply with Prussian demands, which were accompanied by menaces, for the extradition of the refugee professors. As a mark of his extreme displeasure, Frederick William III of Prussia issued a decree prohibiting any Prussian subject from enrolling at the University of Basel, but this was more of a symbolic gesture than an effective one, since the University of Basel was so insignificant at the time (total enrollment in the late 1840s, according to Burckhardt, was twenty-eight students) that no Prussians had been tempted to matriculate there anyway.

Because of all this, the young teachers at the Basel *Gymnasium* and university, many of whom were themselves immigrants from Germany and had been raised on the neohumanist ideas of the celebrated classical scholar Friedrich August Wolf and the scholar-statesman Wilhelm von Humboldt, allowed themselves to imagine that the glories of the ancient Greek city-state were about to be revived on the banks of the Rhine and the Birsig, and that the neohumanist dream of national regeneration through the study of the classical languages and culture, which had suffered a setback in Germany itself, might yet be realized in the old free city of Basel. This was the hope they communicated to their young charges—the sons of the Basel businessmen—at the city's high school and university in the 1820s and 1830s. It was a lesson that marked the most imaginative of them for life and promoted among the leading Basel scholars and writers of the industrial age the uniquely critical view of nineteenth-century modernism and progressivism that characterizes all their work and that made Basel a congenial refuge for others—such as Friedrich Nietzsche or Franz Overbeck—whose criticism of modernism also did not rest on a foundation of traditional conservatism.

Internally, the *Herren* pursued less liberal policies. They supported the guilds well into the nineteenth century, both to protect the local artisans and preserve social peace, and to secure the base of their own political power. Above all, they resisted the demands of the rural districts that they be represented in the Senate in proportion to their population. While they were ready to grant substantial representation to the thirty-six thousand inhabitants of the countryside, they rejected the principle of popular sovereignty and representation based on equal citizens' rights. Since the city proper provided ninety-six percent of the state's tax revenues, they argued, it could not reasonably be expected to yield power to rural squires and small landowners, who supplied only four percent, whose interests were entirely different from their own, and whom they also considered too narrow-minded and parochial to run the state. (The liberal historian and economist Sismondi responded in more or less the same way to the demands of the rural population of Geneva.) The rural districts had achieved full representation during the brief period of the Helvetic Republic, and while there was no return at the Restoration to the status quo ante, the new constitution ensured that rural representation in the Senate would never surpass that of the city.

The ancien regime in Basel, in short, was bourgeois, not aristocratic. As a result, the Revolution of 1830 was not, as elsewhere in Europe, a struggle between the bourgeoisie and a restored aristocracy but an uprising of disenfranchised rural subjects against the restored rule of the burghers of the town. The Basel *Wirren* or Troubles lasted from 1830 until 1833. Compared with present-day Lebanon or Northern Ireland, they might seem a ridiculous, mock-epic affair, in the style of the war between Picrochole and Gargantua over the rival claims of their respective bannock-bakers in Rabelais. Still, the city army lost sixty-five men at the disastrous battle of Pratteln (against five killed on the other side), and the conflict left a legacy of bitterness in Basel, especially toward the Confederation, which intervened and imposed a division of the old canton into the two autonomous half-cantons that still exist today—Basel-city and Basel-country. To the Baselers it seemed that an unwarranted interference by the Confederation in a domestic matter had resulted in the dismemberment of their state. They were also convinced that the Confederation was dominated by the liberals who had come to power in 1830 in most of the other Protestant cantons and that from the beginning it had sided basically with the insurgents. In addition, the financial terms of the settlement were distinctly generous to the rural communities. The city had to appeal to the entire citizenry, for instance, in order to buy back the share of the university allotted by the federal mediators to Basel-country.

The overall effect of the *Wirren* and of the federal mediation, however, was actually to consolidate the power of the elite and to isolate Basel as the only major Protestant city in Switzerland not to have installed a liberal regime in 1830. During the conflict the townspeople, as well as virtually the entire faculty of the university, including those professors who were reputed to be liberals, united behind the elite in defense of the privileges of the city. After the *Kantonstrennung* or division of the canton, the artisans found that they were more dependent on the *Herren* than ever. They were dependent on them as their principal employers and customers, and they were dependent on them to maintain traditional restrictions on the immigrant workers who threatened their livelihood. The artisans were thus a conservative force, in most respects more conservative than the *Herren* themselves. The latter's practical experience and trading interests led them often enough to adopt moderately "progressive" positions, especially in economic matters. In 1844–1845, for instance, realizing that Basel's commercial future was at stake, the *Herren* supported the extension of a railway line from Strasbourg into the city, over the bitter opposition of the artisans who feared the iron horse as the bearer of poisonous presents: an influx of cheaper, French-made goods, dangerous revolutionary and atheistic ideas, strange Catholic

religious practices, and exotic and degenerate pleasures. The authorities had to agree to have a gate constructed over the line at the point
where it penetrated the city wall and to make sure that this gate was
closed and barred every night after the last train had passed through.
Equally, the division of the canton had relieved the patriciate of the
organized and determined opposition to their rule in the rural areas.
Some radicals even charged that the *Herren* had cunningly engi-
neered the division of the canton as the best means of shoring up
their position.

A second effect of the *Wirren* and the division of the canton was
the guarded attitude of at least two generations of Baselers to the
Confederation and above all to any increase in its powers in relation
to the individual member states. During the Sonderbundkrieg of
1847—a civil war that pitted the liberal and progressive Protestant
cantons, which supported a more centralized state with enhanced
federal powers, against the weaker, conservative Catholic cantons,
which favored maximum cantonal autonomy—Basel sympathized
with the Catholic cantons, though it stood by the Confederation, the
Baselers' fear of rebellion and disrespect for law being even greater
than their dislike of centralization. Likewise, though the new constitution of 1848 was easily passed at Basel, a large number of *Rats-
herren* or senators simply stayed away on the day of the vote. Distinguished men from the elite families of Basel helped to build the new
federal rail network, to establish a federal currency, and to promote
the federal postal service. Reduced to the status of a half-canton,
however, the largest and wealthiest city in Switzerland was keenly
aware that it was not a major player in the new federal politics. On
the whole, the attitude of Basel to the post-1848 Confederation was
about as enthusiastic as that of the United Kingdom to the EEC.
The new order was accepted pragmatically as necessary, but everyone
knew it probably spelled the end of the city-republic's long history as
an independent polity. That end came in 1874–1875, with a major
revision of the federal Constitution, which in turn necessitated a new
constitution for Basel. The distinction between the city and the can-

ton was abolished, as were the last remnants of the old guilds, and voting rights were vastly extended to cover all Swiss citizens resident in the city. Basel was finally reduced, as one disgruntled old senator declared, to a mere municipality.[4]

Yet it was in those last years of ever-diminishing autonomy that Basel enjoyed a second Renaissance, a silver age, that made it once again, for a time, a cultural center of European significance. On the threshold of the age of the great nation-states, of economic and political rivalries on a universal scale, of the mass media and mass culture, and of the triumph of rational organization in all areas of life—politics, business, social policies, war, even literature and the arts—a number of writers, scholars, and artists, attached in one way or another to the Basel elite, developed an original, trenchant, though in my view morally and politically ambiguous, critique of modern culture and its shibboleths—"the great optimist-rationalist-utilitarian . . . prejudices of our democratic age," as Nietzsche called them.[5] They were joined by several outsiders who had been hired by the Basel education department, as part of a deliberate policy of applying its meager resources to attract promising younger scholars to the university, so that the city might benefit from their presence for a while before they moved on to better-paying and more prestigious jobs in Germany. Most of these young men did in fact leave. A few, however, the quirky ones, stayed behind, finding conditions in the anachronistic old city-state, if not congenial, then at least more tolerable and tolerant than in the imperial Germany of the *Gründerzeit*. It was Basel's untimeliness, its being politically out of sync with general developments in Europe, that made it the incubator not only of Nietzsche's *Unzeitgemässe Betrachtungen* or *Untimely Meditations* (1873–1876), but of a series of similar works: Bachofen's *Mother-Right* (1861), Burckhardt's *Civilization of the Renaissance in Italy* (1860), and *Greek Cultural History* (posthumous, 1898–1902), Overbeck's *Christianity and Culture* (posthumous, 1919). A brief account of the writers and works of Basel's silver age will help to define the character of the city in its industrial age in the second half of the nineteenth century.

A wealthy private scholar and semirecluse, Johann Jacob Bachofen, heir to the vast Bachofen ribbon fortune, denounced the classical
establishment of his time and its already world-renowned leader,
Theodor Mommsen, for having turned the study of antiquity from
the deeply formative, morally and humanly regenerative activity
imagined by Winckelmann, Wolf, and von Humboldt, into a posi-
tivist scholarly routine and a respectable, secure, and moderately well
remunerated career, and for having ruinously brought it up-to-date,
in Bachofen's own words, with "the pet ideas of Berlin salon-liberal-
ism." As a result, he charged, the ancient cultures were no longer
being studied respectfully by scholars reaching out to understand
them in their own terms, but were being interpreted instead in the
light of the latest liberal values such as political and economic freedom, material prosperity, and social welfare, as if these values had
superseded all others and were thus the measure by which the be-
nighted cultures of the past should be judged.[6] Inevitably, the practi-
tioners of the new philological "science" had proved incapable of
appreciating the interest and importance of ancient myth and had
failed to recognize the essential role of religion in ancient societies
(and, by implication, in all worthwhile societies). The antiquity admired by the Berlin professors and academicians, according to the
wealthy private scholar from Basel, was in fact a tame, sanitized,
modernized version of the real thing, a projection of their own medi-
ocre imaginations and their own situation as salaried professional
civil servants.

Jacob Burckhardt, who—like Bachofen—had studied in Berlin
(Bachofen had been a student of Ranke, Boeckh, and Savigny;
Burckhardt of Ranke, Boeckh, and Droysen) and who belonged to
an even more distinguished Basel family than the Bachofens (the
Burckhardts wielded such influence that Isaac Iselin, the leading
light of the Basel Enlightenment, once referred to them as the
"Medicis" of Basel),[7] repudiated the historical optimism of his teachers, that is to say the belief that history follows a continuous provi-
dential plan, that historical success itself is therefore the ultimate

criterion of value in history (what succeeds is right), and that it is the
task of the historian to decipher the plan as best he can so that mortals may wisely accommodate to it. After living through the disor-
ders in Switzerland in 1845–1847 and the 1848 revolution in Rome,
Burckhardt no longer shared the calm assurance of the Berlin Restoration historians and philosophers that the Revolution was over and
that it had been absorbed and integrated into the continuity of European history, thanks largely to the steadying conservative influence
of the Germanic peoples. To the contrary, he was increasingly convinced that the individualist culture inaugurated by the Italian Renaissance—the culture not only of Florence and Venice, but of Basel,
"the old culture of Europe," as he called it[8]—was fast disintegrating,
nowhere faster than in Bismarckian Prussia itself, where it had never
been well established in the first place, and that the future was a
harsh, new iron age of mass politics, mass culture, and mass armies.
In those circumstance, "it was high time," as he put it, "to free myself
from the bogus-objective recognition of the value of everything,
whatever it may be, and to become thoroughly intolerant."[9]

Instead of accepting the judgment *of* history, as the Restoration
historians proposed to do, the historian's job as Burckhardt now saw
it, was to pronounce judgment *on* history. This was a vision of history not for a time of quiet confidence and restoration but for a time
of growing crisis, and not for professionals or obedient subjects (and
we must remember that in Prussia, the heart of the new historiography, professional historians were state employees or bureaucrats),
but for free citizens, old-fashioned men of independent mind and
means, genuine individuals, such as the educated merchants of Florence—of whom we are given a fine portrait in *The Civilization of the
Renaissance in Italy*—or, for that matter, of humanist and neohumanist Basel, men such as Burckhardt's sixteenth-century ancestor
Theodor Burckhardt, silk-merchant, member of the Kleiner Rat or
cabinet, and *Oberstzunftmeister* or head guildsman of the city, or his
own brother Lucas, who after serving for a quarter of a century as
technical director of his father-in-law's silk-spinning mill retired at

the age of fifty to take up a seat in the senate and devote the years of
his maturity to improving education in the city-state. It is not surprising that in the preface to his first major work, *The Age of Con-
stantine the Great* (1853), Burckhardt announced that he wrote "not
primarily for professional scholars but for thoughtful readers from all
sectors of society." In fact, after *The Civilization of the Renaissance in
Italy* (1860) he virtually stopped publishing altogether, signaling
thereby his refusal to participate in either the new professionalism or
the new literary marketplace, the effects of which on literature and
scholarship he had shrewdly commented on in a series of reports to
the *Basler Zeitung* from Paris in the mid-forties.[10] Nor is it suprising
that the place from which the judgment on history was to be made
was not modern Berlin, the capital of the dynamic new Bismarckian
German state, but eccentric, anachronistic Basel in its *Dreiländerecke*
from where one could look out, just across the frontier, on three
major European countries. Burckhardt's refusal to be considered for
the succession of Ranke in the most prestigious chair of history in
Europe, at the University of Berlin, his determination to "remain at
my post," as he put it,[11] in Basel, were part of a consciously adopted
and consistently followed policy. Finally, the rejection of historical
optimism and progressivism by both Burckhardt and Bachofen led
them to turn from political history to cultural history and anthropology and from traditional narrative forms representing continuity and
orderly succession to mosaic-like montages more appropriate to the
task of representing times of discontinuity and crisis, and the multi-
layered, rather than unitary, character of historical reality.

Franz Overbeck was brought to Basel from Jena in 1870 in re-
sponse to local pressure to have the liberal tendency in modern Protestant theology represented on the faculty. He was a compromise
candidate, the choice of the ruling elite, and only grudgingly accepted from the outset by the reformers. Within barely three years of
his arrival he had published a work that was a scathing critique of
liberal theology, indeed of all theology. Just as Bachofen and Burckhardt rejected the modern transformation of classical studies and

history into a professional, "scientific" activity, insisting instead on their cultural role as part of the education of individual human beings and citizens, Overbeck rejected modern attempts to reconcile religion with scientific scholarship and make it meet the demands of the modern secular intellect. Christianity, he maintained, was an eschatological faith premised on the prophetic announcement of the imminent end of the world. It was a religion of crisis and dramatic decision, not of quiet continuities and compromises. The whole purpose of theology, in contrast, was to ensure the survival of religion and its accommodation to a world that had not in fact ended, to turn religion into an object of professional study. "Theology," in his own remarkable formulation, "is the Satan of religion," and "theologians are traitors to the cause they are to defend," "panderers coupling Christianity and the world," "the Figaros of Christianity," "old washerwomen drowning religion for us in the endlessly flowing stream of their chatter." Moreover, their commitment to the worldly survival of the church has made them "craven worshippers of power in all its forms." All theologians, in Overbeck's pithy phrase, are Jesuits, in the sense that "Jesuitism is Christianity that has become worldly wise."[12] With his polemical *The Christianity of our Present-day Theology*, which appeared in 1873, a year after *The Birth of Tragedy* by his friend and housemate Friedrich Nietzsche and in the same year as the latter's first *Unzeitgemässe* or "Untimely Meditation" on the leader of liberal theology, David Strauss, Overbeck burned his boats and excluded himself from consideration for a post at any major German university. Like many German scholars, he had accepted a position at Basel as a *pis-aller*, planning to stay there only until something better turned up in Germany. In the event, however, as he put it himself, by publishing his essay, he had "embroiled himself in an unresolvable conflict with the dominant theological current in the German Empire and in consequence was condemned to exile."[13] In Basel, on the other hand, though it was soon pretty common knowledge that the new professor of theology was not only a bitter critic of the very subject he had been trained in and appointed to teach, but most likely an atheist into the bargain, the authorities never harassed him. Overbeck taught his courses in church history conscientiously, and enjoyed a high reputation as a historical and textual scholar. In return, the Baselers respected the individual and his private anguish.

In the writings he published in the early years of his occupancy of the chair of Greek at the University of Basel, Friedrich Nietzsche laid out some of the major themes of all his work. In particular, these early writings—notably *The Birth of Tragedy* (1871), the lectures on *The Future of Our Educational Institutions* (delivered as a series of public lectures at Basel between January and March 1872), and the four *Untimely Meditations* (1873–1876)—set forth with great clarity his rejection of nineteenth-century liberalism and progressivism, of modern democratic politics and education, of the growth of state power, and, in general, of the optimistic, rationalist, scientific culture inherted from the Enlightenment. All were well received in Basel. In Germany, in contrast, as is well known, the philological establishment pronounced its anathema on *The Birth of Tragedy* through its spokesman Wilamowitz-Moellendorf (who was also, incidentally, to declare Burckhardt's posthumously published *Greek Cultural History* totally "worthless for science").[14] It was "as if I had committed a crime," Nietzsche himself remarked.[15]

The essence of *The Birth of Tragedy* is a denunciation—not unlike Bachofen's a couple of decades earlier—of the contemporary academic interpretation of Greek culture, a rehabilitation of the tragic and heroic vision of life that, in Nietzsche's view, was held by the pre-Socratic Greeks, and a critique of the "dubious enlightenment," in Nietzsche's own words,[16] by which it had been superseded in the age of Socrates and Euripides. In opposition to modern optimism— "the miserable rationalism and ephemerism of the American way of feeling," as the celebrated neohumanist scholar Friedrich Welcker had put it as early as 1834[17]—Nietzsche proclaimed the harshness of existence and the tragic and dramatic character of life's choices. In addition, in line with the ideas of Wagner, whom he was courting assiduously at the time, *The Birth of Tragedy* was also a call for a reawakened German spirit—still pure and energetic, despite the apparent triumph in 1871 of "mediocrity, democracy, and modern ideas in the pompous guise of empire building"[18]—to bring about a rebirth of tragedy and a restoration of myth to its proper place in culture.

The lectures on education aimed the critique of classical studies in *The Birth of Tragedy* directly at the classical gymnasium and at German education in general. To Nietzsche, as to the neohumanists and to his Basel colleagues, genuine education meant the development, to the highest degree possible, of free and creative individuals. He conceded the value, even the necessity of the *Realschule*, or technical school, with its practical training in the sciences and modern languages, but clearly considered it merely a producer of useful subjects. True leaders, in contrast, can be educated only through the study of Greek language and literature. The alleged failure of the gymnasium in Germany—the central theme of the lectures—thus entails, in Nietzsche's view, a general failure of leadership, a capitulation to the modern forces of democracy and mediocrity. The well-known *Unzeitgemässe* on the "The Use and Abuse of History" obviously strikes an identical note. That Nietzsche's scathing critiques of German education, German philology, and German historical scholarship—all at the height of their world reputation—were made public in Basel is not surprising. Basel had remained, on the whole, faithful not only to the humanist political ideal of the city-state, but to humanist and neohumanist ideas of education. The Baselers still considered a classical education to be a general education for citizens rather than a training for future professionals. For that reason, in fact, the Berlin classical establishment had a rather low opinion of the teaching of Latin and Greek in Basel, judging it backward and amateurish.[19]

Though there were differences among them, especially no doubt between the native Baselers on the one hand and the German immigrants on the other, all the Basel-based critics were sharply opposed to the modern world developing around them, most vividly in the new German Empire, but also, as the letters of both Bachofen and Burckhardt make quite clear, in Basel itself. Under their very eyes, they could observe the old merchant economy and culture being replaced by a more up-to-date and thoroughly rationalized industrial and corporate economy and culture, at the same time as the constitution was being constantly revised in what Burckhardt called an "ultra-democratic" direction.[20] With their repeated denunciations of universal suffrage, the rule of democracy, the invasion of the state into all spheres of life, the bureaucratization of cultural activities, and the development of the mass media, what the Basel critics feared and were determined to resist was a vast cultural shift, as they perceived it, toward a new form of collectivism, in the form of a rationalization of all areas of life: society and the state (substitution of the mass for the individual, of quantitative for qualitative values, together with an unlimited expansion of bureaucracy); business and industry (substitution of the public company, with publicly traded shares and professional managers, for the family-run enterprise, of factory production for artisanal production, of a corporate ethos for an ethos of individual risk and responsibility); war (substitution of military science and weapon technology for individual valor and resourcefulness); and finally culture itself (substitution of market-driven production for the creative work of individual artists).

In their way, the Basel critics were anticipating and warning against what Max Weber was to call the "iron cage," in which modern man has become the prisoner of the very drive toward rational organization that had earlier emancipated him from the sway of tradition. Above all, none of them made their critique of modernity in the name of the feudal and communal Middle Ages, or of Romantic nationalism and populism; they made it in the name of the very individual energies which had rendered the new collectivism possible and were now themselves—the critics claimed—threatened by it. But the individual they had in mind and wished to defend was not the individual as a subject of rights, the abstract moral and legal individual of British and French liberal philosophies. It was the individual as the author of free and creative acts and judgments, the individual as artist and entrepreneur. "Personality," Buckhardt asserted, "is the highest thing that there is." "In all ages," according to Bachofen, "what was truly great was the work of individuals." As for the professor of theology and church history at Basel, he maintained quietly that "Whoever stands truly and firmly on his own two feet in the world must have the courage to stand on nothing. The thorough individualist must be able to do without God. . . . Only without God can he live as a free individual."[21]

Nineteenth-century Basel did not, on the face of it, seem a likely place for four such original and unconventional spirits to congregate. The chief business of the inhabitants was making money and they had little time left over for anything else except church-going and a limited ration of what Bachofen referred to disdainfully as "the so-called higher pleasures."[22] When a friend in Zurich recommended a young visitor from Frankfurt to Bachofen, the latter warned that there were few opportunities for diversion in Basel. The young man should not expect to find in Basel the dancing assemblies that had greatly pleased him in Zurich, he wrote. "He will have to forgo all that sort of thing here. I do not recollect ever hearing of any one dancing in Basel. . . . With the best will in the world, I have nothing to offer the young man but the advice that he not stay here too long. The natives go to bed early and discipline themselves from early youth to have as few needs as possible. A lecture, an interminable symphony concert, and a sermon by [the latest revivalist preacher], voilà tout."[23] Nothing that happened in Basel in the course of the nineteenth century—neither the city's emergence as a major hub of the European railway system, nor its expanding industries, nor even its physical transformation from a small, crowded, unsanitary town imprisoned within its medieval walls into a moderately large city, with well laid out public gardens and avenues where once the walls had stood, or the expansion of its cultural institutions—was of a sort to alter Bachofen's dim view of it. Compared to Mycenean Greece, ancient Etruria, and the other early cultures in which he had buried himself—"mi sono quasi sepolto nei sepolchri," he once said of himself[24]—modern Basel was utterly drab. "One day here is very much like another," he wrote to his niece, who was in the south of France, in 1886. "We get up in the morning, consume four meals, then retire to bed again. If the sun shines we go out, if it rains, we take our umbrellas along, as does everybody else. One day I begin my daily constitutional with the Sankt Alban Vorstadt, next day with the Aeschenvorstadt, the day after with the great Gerbergasse. Every morning I take cocoa, every evening tea.

> Wie intressant, wie intressant
> O du mein herrlich Schweizerland."[25]

Jacob Burckhardt—who, like Bachofen, had studied in Berlin and, like Bachofen, had dreaded returning to Basel—had "been spoiled by Germany," in his own words. For many years, all he wanted to do was go back. "I think of nothing else," he confessed on his return to Basel in 1843.[26] After four years of freedom as a student in Berlin and Bonn he felt keenly the restrictions placed on him in a town where, as a member of one of the most prominent families in the city (even if he belonged to a less well-to-do branch, his father being the chief minister at the cathedral), he was known to everyone and closely observed by everyone, and where business success continued to be rated higher than any other accomplishment. The problem, he explained, was neither his family nor the faculty at the university, where he had been given a modest and poorly remunerated appointment. It was the narrowness and maliciousness of Basel society. "Not a word is ever forgotten or forgiven; scandalmongering such as exists nowhere else spreads poison over everything. . . . It is not good in our day and age when a little hole like this is so turned in on itself."[27] "Out of here! Out of here! That is and will remain my motto," he confided a year later to an old friend from happier student days in Germany.[28] "No decent person can stand it for long here among those purse-proud merchants [*Geldbrozen*]."[29] The future seemed bleak indeed. "In Basel," he explained, "I can expect a life of extreme reserve and politeness; there will be no one I can trust fully, no one I can talk to without constraint. The two or three university teachers in the same position as myself are young gentlemen from the leading families in the city, to whom I would never make the first advances, for you have no idea how grotesque and all-pervasive the Basel reverence for wealth is."[30] Burckhardt's sense of life in Basel was also that of Rudolf Jhering, one of the leading legal scholars of nineteenth-century Germany. Bringing him to the university had been one of the many shrewd coups of the Basel education ministry, but Jhering left after only a few years for a post at Rostock, on the grounds that he could never get used to a city where the leading citizens were defined as those whose names could be written with six zeros after them and where success required greater adeptness at bowing and scraping than a simple north German like himself possessed.[31] Nietzsche, who as a brand new Ph.D., was brought to Basel in 1870 to fill the chair of Greek, complained constantly of the dreariness and oppressiveness of life in the damp, cramped old merchant-city. Basel, he declared later to his friend Overbeck, as his health began to break down, has been "the breeding ground of all my ills."[32]

Yet there had never been a shortage of high-spirited and even adventurous individuals in Basel. The city's prosperity had been built, since the Renaissance, on enterprise and risk-taking, as Burckhardt for one understood clearly when he denounced "the ethos of the times" as "a flight from the risks of business into the arms of the salary-paying state."[33] The Merians who had incurred the wrath of Napoleon because of their "smuggling" and the Geigys who committed their money and their reputation to the newfangled chemical industry in the 1860s and 1870s were no slouches. Who knows what restlessness drove Jacob Burckhardt's uncle to go to Moscow and open up a business there? Basel merchants had always traveled far beyond the narrow confines of their Lilliputian state on business, and the city owed much to loyal citizens who preferred to be somewhere else. A fair number of then had chosen to settle abroad permanently: in Paris, London, Vienna, New York, Rio de Janeiro. Some had brilliant careers in foreign service, such as Burckhardt's great-uncle Emanuel, who was Viceroy of Sicily in 1802 and commander-in-chief of the armies of the kingdom of Naples at the Restoration. One of the most colorful figures of the early years of the nineteenth century, a relative of Burckhardt's and Bachofen's, found a more unusual outlet for his wanderlust. After a period spent learning Arabic in Cambridge, England, Jean-Louis or Johann-Ludwig or John Lewis Burckhardt (he is known by all three names), was sent by an English exploration society to explore the upper Nile. To facilitate his work, Jean-Louis dressed and lived like an Arab, and as he had learned to speak Arabic as fluently as he spoke Baseldytsch or English, he was taken for an Arab, became known throughout the Near East as Sheikh Ibrahim, and on his death from dysentry in 1817, a year before the birth of Jacob Burckhardt, was buried as a Muslim in the Bab el Nasr cemetery outside Cairo. A less drastic way of getting out of Basel was to work for the celebrated Basel *Mission*, a religious organization dedicated to bringing the Word to the people of the Indian subcontinent, the Orient, and Africa, or for the Basel Trading Company, founded in 1859 to help finance the work of the *Mission*. The trading company exported Swiss manufactured goods to the same regions where the *Mission* was active and after paying a minimum dividend of six percent to the shareholders divided whatever profits remained equally among the shareholders and the *Mission*, thus ensuring, with typical Basel scrupulosity, that heaven and earth each got their due.

High-spirited Baselers—artists and intellectuals, obviously, in particular—always had to negotiate a compromise between the demands of individual personality and the conditions set by a small, enclosed, and tightly knit community, which must strictly regulate the behavior and relations of its members for the sake of peace and harmony, between energetic entrepreneurialism and concern for the welfare of a population of traditional artisans. (The celebrated Basel irony—one recalls the "sharp eyes and bad tongues" Burckhardt attributed to the Florentines, almost certainly with his own fellow-countrymen in mind[34]—was no doubt among the instruments used to this end.) Inevitably, there were casualties. Some, like the painter Arnold Böcklin, spent their entire lives in exile. But even for those who successfully achieved a modus vivendi with the city, periods of escape seem to have been a minimum requirement for survival. After they returned definitively to Basel, Burckhardt and Bachofen, for instance, made frequent trips to Germany, France, England, and above all Italy—a refuge for both not only from Basel but from modernity in general. Bachofen was torn between—on the one hand—the attraction of another, more glorious and heroic way of life, which he discovered in Mycenean Greece, in ancient Etruria, in the Rome of the early kings, and, in his mature years, in the societies of Africa and Oceania, and—on the other—fear of his own imagination and restlessness, of his desire to *vagari*, as he put it himself,[35] between Basel as a place of exile—*terra aspera et tristis*, as he said, adapting Tacitus[36]—the very essence of the modern world, with its railway cuttings, wailing engines, factory chimneys, and new joint-stock credit banks, and Basel as a place of refuge, a familiar anachronistic old place to withdraw to and hunker down in, the "sulking corner" of Europe, as the upbeat German nationalist historian Treitschke called it.[37] On one occasion, he tells of falling deathly sick while exploring antiquities in the heat and sun of the south of France and of coming back to damp, grey Basel as to a "liebes regnerisches Schützenvaterland"—a dear, wet, secure fatherland.[38] A couple of decades ago, the historian and diplomat Carl Jacob Burckhardt and his friend the art historian Christoph Bernoulli—both expatriate Baselers living in Paris—pondered why the city republic had been, like Plato's, so inimical to poets, what it was about it that stultified lively minds, such as one *Altbasler*, evoked by Carl Burckhardt, who had been a live wire in the brilliant circles of the Schlegels and the

Humboldts in Berlin in the 1820s, but who, on returning to his native city withdrew for the rest of his life into silent retirement. "He suffered a Basel fate," Carl Burckhardt commented, "a fate of renunciation."[39]

Adventure and renunciation, "personality" and conformity—these appear to have been the two poles of life in Basel for centuries: that is to say, openness to the world and withdrawal into the cocoon of community, experiment and tradition, criticism and prudent acceptance, transgression of limits (Bachofen's *vagari*) and acceptance of them. The tension of being positioned between those two poles appears to have been what distinguished the native-born Basel critics of modernity—Bachofen and Burckhardt—from the visitors—Nietzsche and Overbeck. There were differences between the two Baselers of course, and it even seems somehow characteristic of Basel that though they knew each other and each other's work well, though their families were connected, and though they lived within a stone's throw of each other—the millionaire hermit in the opulent obscurity of his grand house on the Münsterplatz, in the very center of town, and the modest college teacher in his unpretentious rooms on the Sankt Albanvorstadt—they appear to have had only guarded contacts with each other.[40]

But the differences between the two Baselers were essentially differences in temperament, family background, and material circumstances. Basically both men shared a deep-seated skepticism not only about liberal ideas of progress and democracy, which they both saw as the harbingers of socialism and a new collectivism, but about virtually all blueprints for radical change or social reform. Both were convinced that there was nothing to do but ride out the coming time of disasters, while standing up in complete isolation, if necessary, for what they judged to be right and preserving what they could of the culture that was doomed. In any case, human existence, both were convinced, did not admit of perfection. If excessive development of the state, for instance, usually results in the impoverishment of culture, as Burckhardt argued, it is no less true that culture can develop to the point where it corrodes the bonds that hold communities together. Everything is a matter of degree and of fine tuning, of balancing competing values and equally justified claims. "There are no golden ages in the past or in the future," Burckhardt stated firmly.[41] Consistent with this resolute realism, Burckhardt rejected the daemonic. "If you truly believe you are a daemonic nature," he wrote to a young friend, "I ask one thing of you, and that is that you never, not for a single instant, find satisfaction in that fact." It requires no great effort to be negative and critical, he added. "Avoid it: it is easy to destroy, and very difficult to rebuild."[42]

Burckhardt vehemently rejected Nietzsche's reading of his own work as a glorification of human energy and artistry "beyond good and evil." "I have never been an admirer of *Gewaltmenschen* and *Outlaws* in history," he protested, "and have on the contrary held them to be *flagella dei* [scourges of God]."[43] Even if matters are not as simple as Burckhardt lets on here,[44] it is certainly true that he frequently evoked a very different kind of hero from Nietzsche's superman: Demosthenes, for instance, warning of the threat to the independent Greek cities from the aggressive new Macedonian state of Philip II, and standing up obstinately against what Droysen and the German historical school reproached him for not welcoming as the inevitable and therefore proper course of history;[45] or the modest, austere, profoundly conservative abbot, later known as St. Severin, who, from the monasteries he had founded along the valleys of the Danube and the Inn, on the frontiers of the disintegrating Roman Empire, continued to preach the word and to minister to his flock until his last breath, doing his bit to preserve the culture of antiquity in a time of chaos, so that it could be picked up again and built upon in better times.[46]

The qualities Burckhardt admired in the Athenian orator and in the Italian-born abbot—dedication to principle, combined with pragmatic activism and solidarity with their fellow humans, above all

perseverance in the face of the tide of history itself—are in all proba-
bility not only those he liked to think were his own, but those that he
associated with his native city at its best and that made it, in his eyes,
a last outpost of humanist values in a world bent on their destruction.

✦ ✦ ✦

Cities are defined not only by their complex, endlessly shifting em-
pirical reality but by their more enduring symbolic significance—
which is related to that reality, but not identical with it. From the
time of Erasmus to the time of Burckhardt, from its golden age in
the fifteenth and sixteenth centuries to its silver age in the nineteenth, the symbolic significance of Basel has remained surprisingly
constant. Because of its peculiar geographical and historical position,
Basel has been faithful to its bourgeois and humanist tradition. It has
consistently stood for a judicious mixture of principle and pragma-
tism, individual enterprise and social cohesion, adaptation to the
new and fidelity to the old. Its leaders have always had to juggle
conflicting claims and to acknowledge opposing points of view.
Clear decisions and final solutions have not been the Baselers' style.[47]
They have neither opted out of history nor swum carelessly with the
tide. Thus, in its heyday, the University of Basel could not come
down decisively on the side of either the nominalists or the realists
in the greatest debate of the time, but permitted both parties to rep-
resent their views to the students. Even in the city's silver age, the
very writers to whom—as we have seen—the most relevant literary
model for their own time was not the progressively evolving narrative
of liberal historiography but a stalled account of crisis, tried to avoid
overly dramatizing this situation in the Nietzschean manner. More
recently, constitutional changes introduced since the 1870s have
forced constant compromises between the interests of the elite—
who remain influential not only in all the city's cultural institutions
and in its wealthy philanthropic foundations, but in its finance and
industry too—and popular pressures for social-welfare legislation

that led to the dominance of socialist administrations between 1935 and 1950 and to the election of a communist President of the Senate in 1939. The catastrophic chemical spill into the Rhine from the Sandoz plant in 1986 again challenged the city to reconcile the immense power of the industries on which its prosperity is founded with the authority of the city government and the general welfare of the citizens.

It is not surprising that when a young Nazi historian, writing in 1939, identified the two Germanic mercantile civilizations at the head and the mouth of the Rhine—Switzerland and Holland—as the most insidious and obdurate enemies of the new Germany because of their liberalism, their neutralism, and their persistent avoidance of radical political decisions in favor of cautious compromises, he awarded the palm to "die stolze Basilea" [the haughty old republic of Basel]. Basel's historical existence as a border city, he declared, "had developed in it the ability to slither and wriggle around in the cracks between particular powers to such a degree of virtuosity that every artistic or intellectual production that comes out of it is marked by neutralism."[48] Curiously enough, this vision was shared by Karl Barth, the celebrated modern theologian, who gave up a university chair in Germany to return to his native Basel after running foul of the Nazis. In his classic *History of Protestant Theology in the Nineteenth Century*, Barth—himself, like Overbeck, whom he much admired, a theologian of crisis—drew a portrait of the ordinary Basel theologian that we can take as a portrait of the city itself.

> The Basel theologian is from the start and in all essentials conservative, a basically shy man of the *quieta non movere* ["let sleeping dogs lie," or "don't fix it if it ain't broke"], and that will always emerge somewhere in his person. At the same time, however, he has his secret, almost sympathetic delight in the radicalism and extravagance of others, for instance of all kinds of excited foreigners whom, from David Joris [a sixteenth century Anabaptist] to Nietzsche and Overbeck he has eagerly welcomed within his walls for the contrast they

provide. While finding them frightfully interesting, however, he will hesitate to make them his own. A mild humanistic skepticism that is, so to speak, inborn inoculates him against both Catholicism and excessively strict Calvinist orthodoxy. A practical wisdom, acquired by careful observation, protects him for diverging too much to the left or to the right. So he settles down somewhere in the middle of these extremes, devoting himself to a little free-thinking and indulging equally quietly in a little pious enthusiasm, while outwardly in all circumstances presenting the picture of a sound union of freedom and moderation, affirming and striving for nothing impractical, assuming ironically the presence of eccentricity whenever he runs into excessive insistence on principle, always inclined to attribute disagreement to a mere dispute about words, and to leave opening and closing statements to others.[49]

NOTES

1. "W.A. Mozart, 1756–1956," in *Religion and Culture: Essays in Honor of Paul Tillich*, ed. Walter Leibrecht (Harper, New York: Harper 1959), p. 78.

2. See the extraordinarily rich recent work by Alfred Berchtold, *Bâle et l'Europe: une histoire culturelle*, 2 vols. (Lausanne: Payot, 1990).

3. Maurice Lévy-Leboyer, *Les Banques européennes et l'industrialisation internationale dans la première moitié du XIXe siècle* (Paris: Presses Universitaires de France, 1964), pp. 349–50, 450–51, 469, 471, 592, 705n; Max Ikle, *Die Schweiz als internationaler Bank = und Finanzplatz* (Zurich: Orell Füssli, 1970), pp. 21–23; H. C. Peyer, "Basel in der Züricher Wirtschaftsgeschichte," *Basler Zeitschrift für Geschichte und Altertumskunde* 69 (1969): 223–37.

4. See Werner Kaegi, *Jacob Burckhardt: eine Biographie* (Basel: Benno Schwabe & Co., 1947–1977), 7: 124.

5. Friedrich Nietzsche, *The Birth of Tragedy; The Genealogy of Morals*, trans. Francis Golffing (Garden City, N.Y.: Doubleday, 1956), p. 9.

6. Letter to Heinrich Meyer-Ochsner, January 24, 1862, J. J. Bachofen, *Gesammelte Werke*, ed. Karl Meuli (Basel: Benno Schwabe & Co., 1943– ; in progress), vol. 10 (correspondence), pp. 251–52. (All translations by L. Gossman, unless otherwise indicated.) See also L. Gossman, "Orpheus

Philologus: Bachofen versus Mommsen on the Study of Antiquity," *Transactions of the American Philosophical Society* 73, pt. 5 (1983); Gossman, "Basle, Bachofen and the Critique of Modernity in the Second Half of the Nineteenth Century," *Journal of the Warburg and Courtauld Institutes* 47 (1984):136–85; Gossman, "Antimodernism in Nineteenth Century Basle: Franz Overbeck's Antitheology and J. J. Bachofen's Antiphilology," *Interpretation* 16 (1989):359–89.

7. *Tagebuch Isaak Iselin* (ms.), August 27, 1755, quoted in Kaegi, *Jacob Burckhardt*, 1: 38.

8. "Die Bildung Alteuropas," letter to Hermann Schauenburg, February 28, 1846, in Jacob Burckhardt, *Briefe*, ed. Max Burckhardt (Basel: Benno Schwabe & Co., 1949–1980; in progress), 2: 210.

9. Letter to Paul Heyse, August 13, 1852, *Briefe*, 3:161.

10. See the summary of these reports, which appeared on September 18, 1844, November 30, 1844, September 23, 1845, and October 8, 1845, in Kaegi, *Jacob Burckhardt*, 2: 432–35.

11. Letter to Bernhard Kugler, August 9, 1874, *Briefe*, 5: 237.

12. Franz Overbeck, *Christentum und Kultur: Gedanken und Anmerkungen zur heutigen Theologie*, ed. C. A. Bernoulli (Basel: Benno Schwabe & Co., 1919), pp. 13, 124, 236, 242, 253, 273–74.

13. *Über die Christlichkeit unserer heutigen Theologie*, 2d ed. (Leipzig: Wissenschaftliche Buchgesellschaft, 1903; repr. 1981), p. 169.

14. *Griechische Tragödien*, trans. Ulrich von Wilamowitz-Moellendorf, 5th ed. (Berlin: Weidmannsche Buchhandlung, 1907), "Vorwort" (1899), 2: 7.

15. Letter to Erwin Rohde, October 25, 1872, in Friedrich Nietzsche, *Briefwechsel*, ed. G. Colli and M. Montinari (Berlin and New York: de Gruyter, 1975–1984), pt. II, 3: 71.

16. Nietzsche, *Birth of Tragedy*, p. 82.

17. Letter of December 13, 1834, quoted in Max Hoffmann, *August Boeckh: Lebensbeschreibung und Auswahl aus seinem wissenschaftlichen Briefwechsel* (Leipzig: B. G. Teubner, 1901), p. 181.

18. Nietzsche, *Birth of Tragedy*, p. 138.

19. See the recollections of the poet Carl Spitteler, who was a student in Basel: "Böcklin, Burckhardt, Basel," in his *Gesammelte Werke* (Zurich: Artemis Verlag, 1945–1958), 6: 163–65. See also Kaegi, *Jacob Burckhardt*, 4: 120–26.

20. Letter to Bernhard Kugler, August 9, 1874, *Briefe*, 5: 237.

21. Burckhardt as quoted by James Hastings Nichols, Preface to J. Burckhardt, *Force and Freedom: Reflections on History* (New York: Pantheon, 1943), p. 17; J. J. Bachofen, *Griechische Reise*, ed. Georg Schmidt

(Heidelberg: Richard Weissbach, 1927), p. III; Overbeck, *Christentum und Kultur*, p. 286.

22. Letter to Heinrich Meyer-Ochsner, December 26, 1858, in Bachofen, *Gesammelte Werke* vol. 10 (correspondence), p. 185.

23. Letter to Heinrich Meyer-Ochsner, November 1861, *Gesammelte Werke*, 10: 248.

24. Letter to Count Giovanni Gozzadini, November 5, 1867, *Gesammelte Werke*, 10: 391–92.

25. Letter of April 8, 1887, *Gesammelte Werke*, 10: 547.

26. Letter to Gottfried Kinkel, November 26, 1843, *Briefe*, 2: 52.

27. Letter to Gottfried Kinkel, November 24, 1843, *Briefe*, 2: 51.

28. Letter to Johanna Kinkel, January 29, 1844, *Briefe*, 2: 81.

29. Letter to Gottfried and Johanna Kinkel, September 11, 1846, *Briefe*, 3: 36.

30. Letter to Gottfried Kinkel, August 20, 1843, *Briefe*, 2: 34–35.

31. Letter to Bachofen, June 22, 1846, in "Unbekannte Briefe R. von Jherings aus seiner Frühzeit 1846–1852," *Zeitschrift für schweizerisches Recht*, new series, 53 (1934): 38.

32. Postcard to Overbeck, April 3, 1879, in Nietzsche, *Briefwechsel*, ed. Colli and Montinari, pt. II, 5: 402.

33. Letter to Von Preen, April 13, 1882, *Briefe*, 8: 32.

34. *Civilisation of the Renaissance in Italy*, trans. S.G.C. Middlemore, with an introduction by Benjamin Nelson and Charles Trinkhaus (New York: Harper, 1958), p. 168.

35. Letter to Meyer-Ochsner, March 16, 1862, *Gesammelte Werke*, 10: 255: "I cannot tell you what a desire to *vagari* is brewing again within me." Cf. letter to the same, July 31, 1856, *Gesammelte Werke*, 10: 149: "With me there is always a terrible danger that once the anchor has been raised, the shore is soon left far behind, and the ship steers an ever wilder course toward unfamiliar lands."

36. Letter to Carl von Savigny, August 16, 1854, *Gesammelte Werke*, 10: 136. See also letters to the Italian scholar Agostino Gervasio of January 6, 1848, 10: 80 ("coelum horridum, terra aspera . . . domi ut ita dicam exul") and January 25, 1851, 10: 117 (". . . Basileam, horridam terram et asperam").

37. Letter to Overbeck, October 28, 1873, in *Heinrich Treitschkes Briefe*, ed. Max Cornelius (Leipzig: S. Hirzel, 1914–1920), 3: 375.

38. Letter to Meyer-Ochsner, July 12, 1861, *Gesammelte Werke*, 10: 235.

39. Carl Jacob Burckhardt, "Basel" in his *Gesammelte Werke* (Bern, Munich, Vienna: Scherz, 1971), 5: 381–88.

40. Bachofen, who, at the age of thirty, resigned from a chair of law at the university after a fracas over his appointment, gave up a seat in the senate, and virtually withdrew from public life in Basel for the rest of his life, seems to have reveled in his embitterment; Burckhardt, in contrast, to have been determined not to yield to resentment or despair. Instead, Burckhardt tried to follow the example of his beloved Italian teacher at the Basel *Pädagogium*, Luigi Picchioni, to whom *The Civilization of the Renaissance* is dedicated, and whom he admired for his resiliency, his youthful high spirits, and his warm humanity in the face of successive political disappointments and a life spent largely in exile. (Picchioni had been a carbonaro in the second decade of the century and had had to flee Italy under sentence of death; in 1848 he had returned to Italy to serve briefly as a volunteer with the Milanese in the unsuccessful uprising against Austria.)

41. *Historische Fragmente*, ed. Emil Dürr (Stuttgart: Koehler, 1957), p. 3.

42. Letter to Albert Brenner, a student from Basel, March 16, 1856, *Briefe*, 3: 248–49.

43. Letter to Ludwig Pastor, January 23, 1896, in Otto Markwart, *Jacob Burckhardt: Persönlichkeit und Jugendjahre* (Basel: Benno Schwabe & Co., 1920), p. 44.

44. Many elements of a radical right-wing ideology seem to be already in place in Burckhardt, including anti-Semitism, endemic until recently in Basel as in many other parts of Switzerland. (There is a moving passage in a letter from Karl Barth to Friedrich Wilhelm Marquardt—September 5, 1967 [*Letters 1961–1968*, trans. G.W. Bromiley (Edinburgh: T. and T. Clark, 1981), pp. 261–63]—where the eminent theologian acknowledges feelings of anti-Semitism, while at the same time reproving them and expressing envy, admiration, and relief that his children are free of them.) Even though, on at least one occasion, Basel offered sanctuary to Jews fleeing a pogrom in Alsace—an event that prompted the Jews of Alsace to include a prayer for the city of Basel in their synagogue services—Jews were consistently refused rights of residency. To Burckhardt in particular, Jews represented the very essence of the *nuova gente*, the rootless opportunists and career academics, the mass-media barons, and the producers and consumers of "demi-culture" that he hated. In his monumental biography of Burckhardt, Werner Kaegi does his best to banalize and minimize Burckhardt's anti-Semitism—since in the postwar period when Kaegi was writing, anti-Semitism had become unacceptable—but he is not persuasive. While Burckhardt's anti-Semitism is obviously not that of Chamberlain or Rosenberg, it is not innocent.

What preserved Burckhardt from the shrillness and excess that made him increasingly uneasy in his young friend and admirer Nietzsche seems to me to have been culture and habit, rather than thought or principle: his patrician background, his urbanity and good manners, his upbringing and basic decency, his roots in a tradition of caution and skepticism, his unshakable sense of local, class, and family identity, of being, after all, a Burckhardt—his deep investment, in short, in the existing bourgeois order. Others who were less fortunate, poorer, from less cultivated backgrounds, and—because of that—more subject to feelings of humiliation and resentment, lacked the inhibiting cultural and character traits that allowed Burckhardt to resist the tide he himself did nothing to arrest. Whereas the Basel patrician was able to adopt a detached, ironical, estheticizing attitude to forces he knew were dangerous and disruptive, a gifted and troubled young man from obscure and humble origins, such as Christoph Steding—the Nazi historian mentioned at the end of this essay—could not. Steding had studied in Basel. Who knows what humiliations, what sense of alienation and inferiority experienced in the closed and highly stratified society from which, as we saw, Jhering had fled long before, and from which Burckhardt himself suffered, aggravated his dissaffection from a social order he perceived as repressive and exclusive, encouraged him to embrace National Socialism, and provoked, finally, his six hundred-page diatribe against "die stolze Basilea"?

45. In a public lecture given at Basel and reported by Kaegi, *Jacob Burckhardt*, 2: 44–45.

46. See letter to Andreas Heusler, March 4, 1848 (*Briefe*, 3: 103). In the 1850s Burckhardt gave a public lecture at Basel on St. Severin, and at the end of his life, in a letter to Otto Markwart of November 15, 1893, he again referred to St. Severin, "for me, one of the greatest of mortals" (quoted in Markwart, *Jacob Burckhardt*, pp. 44–45).

47. See a letter from Karl Barth to Eduard Thurneysen, February 16, 1923, in *Karl Barth–Eduard Thurneysen Briefwechsel, 1921–1930* (Karl Barth, *Briefe*, vol. 2 [Zurich: Theologischer Verlag, 1974], pp. 143–45.

48. Christoph Steding, *Das Reich und die Krankheit der europäischen Kultur* (Hamburg: Hanseatische Verlagsanstalt, 1942), pp. 42–43, 203, and *passim*.

49. Karl Barth, *Protestant Theology in the Nineteenth Century* (London: S.C.M. Press, 1972), p. 145 (translation slightly modified).

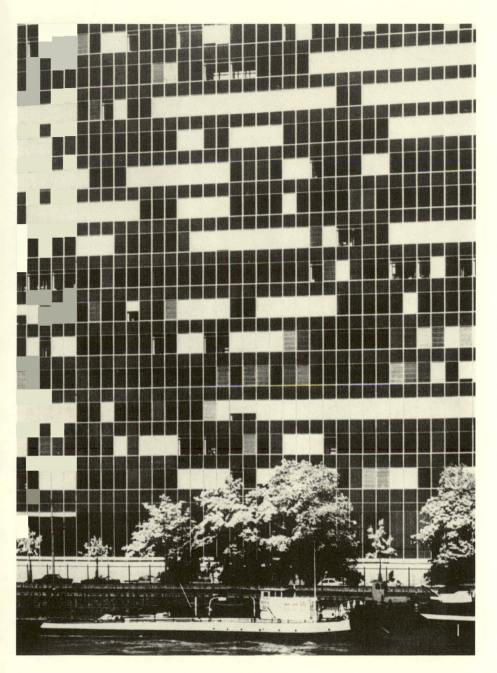

6. Basel